Helen Post

A search for freedom

Helen Post

A search for freedom

ISBN/EAN: 9783337278717

Printed in Europe, USA, Canada, Australia, Japan

Cover: Foto ©Lupo / pixelio.de

More available books at **www.hansebooks.com**

A

Search for Freedom

By Helen Wilmans

SEA BREEZE, FLORIDA:
FREEDOM PUBLISHING COMPANY
1898

CONTENTS.

	PAGE.
CHAPTER I.—Chapter One Introduces Two Important Characters—Little Aunt Mary and Gus	5
CHAPTER II.—"Smartest Youngun 'at Ever Lived, B'gosh"	27
CHAPTER III.—A Love Letter	53
CHAPTER IV.—The Goodest Little Boy That Ever Lived	73
CHAPTER V.—Brother Findlay Comes to Town	88
CHAPTER VI.—At a Catholic School	103
CHAPTER VII.—The Dalton Episode	118
CHAPTER VIII.—Lloyd, Billy Wilkes, and Sally Start a Circus	139
CHAPTER IX.—The Story of Ten Little Hats	161
CHAPTER X.—Two Offers of Marriage	180
CHAPTER XI.—A Most Worshipful Hero	199
CHAPTER XII.—School Again	215
CHAPTER XIII.—A Boy Lover	233
CHAPTER XIV.—"Fearfully" in Love	251
CHAPTER XV.—A Broken Idol	266
CHAPTER XVI.—The Fetters Are Falling	282
CHAPTER XVII.—In the Reform Movement	297
CHAPTER XVIII.—A Glimpse of the Promised Land	313
CHAPTER XIX.—All Is Mind: the Substance of Which Worlds Are Made Is Mental Substance: Thought Has Built the Visible Universe	326
CHAPTER XX.—Coming to Florida	340
CHAPTER XXI.—A Vision of the Dauntless "I"	354

A SEARCH FOR FREEDOM.

CHAPTER I.

CHAPTER ONE INTRODUCES TWO IMPORTANT CHARACTERS—LITTLE AUNT MARY AND GUS.

Not long ago I read the opening chapter in the autobiography of a distinguished literary woman. Every page of it and every word of it were spent in apologizing for the egotism that must of necessity be apparent in works that naturally embody the personality of the writer. As I continued to read it I wondered if there was anything on earth quite so weak, and often so insincere as an apology. It is a confession of shame, either real or hypocritical; and why should one be ashamed of his personality, or why should it be considered the proper thing to affect shame?

A book may be of infinite worth, but the personality

back of it is what makes it so; and it is the glimpses of this personality filtering through the book that give it its vital power to enthrall our imagination and arouse our affection.

I had a lesson on the subject of apologies that taught me enough to avoid them forever. I lived in California and my neighbors were farmers and poor people. Nevertheless, we were social and entertained each other the best we could. It was a matter of pride with us to give good dinners to each other; and a dinner without fried chicken, mashed potatoes and hot biscuit, preserves and pound cake, golden coffee and rich cream, and many other cherished delicacies, was really not respectable—so rigorous was our social code. Moreover, at these dinners the hostess usually indulged in apologies for the many deficiencies supposed to be apparent; thus leaving the impression that she could have done a great deal better if she had been informed of our coming beforehand.

I was returning the visit of one of my neighbors one day when I learned the lesson of being above making an apology ever again—except for a wrong done, or a mistake committed. The lady I was visiting went out to prepare dinner, and was quite a long time about it. This time must have been devoted to her perplexity; it certainly was not given to her dinner, since she had nothing but beans which evidently had been boiling for an hour before my arrival. There was one cup of coffee, and but one. No doubt it was warmed over from breakfast; and it was given to me. Her tablecloth was very white, and everything, though exceedingly poor, was neat. She was a Southern woman, tall and dark and weather-beaten in appearance. In accordance with Southern custom she stood up while the family were at dinner. At first I could scarcely believe it possible that what I saw before me was really the entire dinner; simply beans seasoned with a small piece of pork, and the one cup of coffee. But this was all; and there stood the lady with a palm leaf fan in her hand fanning us while we ate. Not one word of excuse did she offer, though there was a look in her eyes that went straight to my heart and left an indelible impression.

At this time, after the lapse of so many years, all I

can get of that impression is a sense of womanliness beyond the power of words to describe. There was reticence there, and the pride of many generations of culture, all imprisoned within her own individuality, and never to be betrayed by one word that might seem to reflect discredit upon it—that sacred consciousness of beautiful self-hood so plainly visible through the pathos of her eyes and the gentle dignity of her movements.

Appearances might confess her poverty, but she would not. They might confess the fact that her husband was one of the most trifling, dissipated men in the community, but she would not. They might speak volumes of her degraded and unlovely life, but she would not. Her native queenhood was inviolable. She felt it to be so; and what was more, I felt it too; and I know to this day that what I dined upon was not beans, but the ambrosia of the gods, and served by one of them.

And so in the papers I am writing, I shall give the best I have without apology. It will be the best I have, because it will be the "I" that I am giving. In giving my "I" I shall disclose the "I" in you who read, for we are all off one piece. And oh! a wonderful thing is the "I," whether it is my "I" or your "I"; such a beautiful thing; such a majestic thing; and so varied in its phases; and for all the variations of it I am so thankful and so glad. No two pages in any life history alike, and yet each one so vital, so alive!

This aliveness! It is this which gives an autobiography its charm. The individual is all there; present in his own words. He brings himself with him in every page. And this is saying wonders; for if a person brings himself into your presence, he has brought a condensed world there for your inspection; and if you are anything of a naturalist you cannot help but be interested.

For my part I am a natural-born naturalist, and like to see the world through many different kinds of glasses; so when, instead of giving me the glass of her own personality to see the world in, the lady of whom I first spoke spent twenty pages in apologizing for the self-hood of herself, my interest was destroyed and I read no more.

But this work I am now writing is not going to be a real autobiography, but only a sketchy sort of reminiscence. I may write away quite consecutively for several chapters, and then jump whole years; and perhaps I may go back to these neglected years to pick incidents out of them later on. At all events I will do the best I can to show how I cut a trail for myself, through jungles of errors and mistakes, from a land of bondage to one of comparative freedom; a freedom that continually grows more free, and will no doubt keep doing so while I remain an honest searcher for truth.

I wonder if there are many children who feel themselves to be prisoners all through their childish years? This is the way I felt. I used to hear my parents say, "What a good time the youngsters have; especially Helen! Surely, childhood is the happiest period of life."

Then I would ponder this oft-repeated expression, and sometimes it dismayed me. If childhood was the happiest part, what must the rest be? For I was not happy. With everything to make me happy I was still quietly unhappy. I felt myself hampered and restrained. There was an internal restlessness, as if some imprisoned thing were trying to find expression through me, and could not.

And yet I was more free than ordinary children in that age and under similar conditions; for my mother did not hold me in check overmuch, though at the time I thought she did. There were very few outward restrictions about me; but I carried with me always the fettered feeling of one who wears unseen bonds. When I played childish games with others of my own age, my playing and my enjoyment seemed a pretense to me. If I had been an old person indulging in infantile sports I should not have felt more out of place than I did. I actually had a sense of shame in doing it; it all seemed so foolish; so puerile.

And yet I was not precocious. I think my brain was rather sluggish, and I was very indolent. I was heavy in my movements and disinclined to action; but I doubt if a healthier child was ever born.

My parents considered me thoughtful because I spent so much of my time sitting or lying around quietly, and with an appearance of being in a deep revery over something or other.

But in this matter they flattered me, for I cannot recall that I ever thought much in those days. But I do recall that I always seemed on the verge of thinking, and that the thoughts eluded me. Not that I made an effort to hold them fast, for I did not. I seemed to feel that I would be able to think some day and could easily wait.

It was as if something were ripening in my brain, but was not then ripe. If there is anything in reincarnation it might be believed that some old spirit had taken possession of my baby head, and found difficulty in adapting itself to such crude, unmanageable substance as existed there.

This doctrine of reincarnation is a very strange one. It involves more than its advocates seem to see in it; but perhaps I do not really know what they do see. At all events I shall not discuss the subject here, but will try to pin myself down to the matter in hand. For it seems to me that if only one person, who, from the first, has followed faithfully in the direction of more intellectual light, which means more freedom, will give a history of the road he has travelled, and the obstacles he has overcome, it will be a more practical help to other searchers for truth than the mere cold enunciation of principles, divorced from the personality that gave rise to them.

I recall how in my baby years I rarely accepted the opinions of others, but sought to get at the cause of things myself. For instance, I was one day in the carriage with my parents on the road to Carmi, where my grandfather and grandmother lived. I could not have been more than three years old at the time. I was beset with anxiety for fear the horses would make a mistake, and not take us there; so I asked my mother if there was any danger on this score. She said "No; that my father was holding the reins that guided the horses, and that they would surely go right."

This did not appear reasonable to me, and I kept thinking and thinking. After a time I came to the conclusion that on the previous evening the stable man must have told the horses that they were to take us to Carmi the next day. I found no difficulty in believing this, and all my anxiety was removed. I suppose I must have manifested a good deal of this kind of reasoning in my early childhood, and that its fallacy taught me to distrust my reasoning powers. Certain it is, I became in time the obedient recipient of all manner of beliefs that poured in on me from other people, and my own reasoning faculties were dormant for many years. If it had not been for this I should have escaped circumstances that almost tortured the life out of me.

Evidently I was a child who sought for the cause in all the events that passed under my observation; but because in these early efforts I made such mistakes as I have spoken of, I became discouraged, and began to doubt my ability to discriminate between right and wrong. This lifted me off the base of my own individuality, and made a mere dependent of me so far as my judgment was concerned.

If my natural tendency to do my own thinking had been properly directed, instead of being ridiculed and crushed, I should never have become the agonized victim of church dogma, and submitted to the awful belief of an endless hell for those whose reasoning powers prevented them from accepting unproven creeds. At this time I know that it was not I who accepted these creeds. The "I" in me had been set aside, and the fears and false beliefs of the world had been substituted. It was these fears, these false beliefs that spoke and acted through my bodily organism for years. And the awakening, when at last it came, was as if I had been lost to myself for an age, and had been suddenly, through a certain overt act which I will tell of further on, restored to myself.

We were a very large family of children, and our father and mother had been mere children themselves when they were married. I was the second child and the eldest girl. I was the laziest little imp that ever lived. If my poor young mother sent me to wash the dishes, I would slip off and go to the garret or somewhere else, and there lying on the floor or the grass I would read "Arabian Nights" the entire afternoon. I knew I would get whipped when I went to supper, but I did not seem to be afraid of a whipping, from which I infer that mother's whippings were very mild.

And, indeed, they must have been. I remember now how the slightest bit of wit from us would make her laugh. She was a glorious laugher, and she evidently thought that we were the smartest children that the world had produced. Gus, my elder brother, and I used to get together and rehearse something that we considered funny previous to entering her presence, after we had been disobedient and expected a whipping; and this expedient was usually successful.

But I have an idea that mother whipped Gus oftener and harder than she did me. He was more afraid of a whipping than I was, and I was more afraid for him, and early learned to screen him by no end of deceptions.

This whipping we all know to be a very great mistake now, but at that time it was thought to be a terrible thing not to whip children. The people really believed they were earning some great future reward, both for themselves and the children, by bringing them up in fear of the lash. Poor Gus must have been a more timid child than I was; and it is the timid children who are most easily ruined by this rough method of punishment. And yet Gus was not ruined.

I remember one time when mother had sent us all to Sunday school, and when I made her believe I had the colic and remained at home (I always hated Sunday school), that long before it was time for the children to return, Gus rushed into the sitting room exclaiming, "Oh! mother, mother, it's in the lesson to-day where old Solomon—and he is the wisest old fellow that ever lived—said, '*spoil the rod and spare the child*,' and now you can't whip us any more forever."

I think mother felt a genuine heart pang as she looked in the boy's bright, earnest, handsome face. She put her arms around him and told him of his mistake. But she had to get the Bible and read it with him before he was convinced. He was greatly disappointed, and I suppose he thought there was no help for him but in being good—a monotonous alternative.

Mother had the belief that children must not be praised; that praise would ruin them. So she told us of our faults and failings, and used such persistent energy in destroying everything like vanity in us, that I really believe she would have crushed every one of us to an extent that would have rendered us unfit for meeting men and women as equals in later life, if it had not been for a "special providence" in the shape of "little aunt Mary."

Little aunt Mary was two years older than Gus, and four years older than I was. She was the youngest child of her mother, who was dead, and she owed her special rearing to the indulgent influence of her father, one of the most magnificent specimens of manhood that ever lived. Oh! if I only had time to write a character sketch of this loving-hearted, great, kingly soul, I could put an inspiration in it that no personal experiences of my own have power to evoke.

The way grandfather brought up little aunt Mary was to let her bring herself up. They did not live with us, but came often and made long visits; and then there were months at a time when grandfather was absent on business, when little aunt Mary was put under mother's care. This little aunt was a phenomenon. Nobody's opinion had the slightest effect on her character or conduct. For this reason I think she may have been very annoying to her elders. She did not seem to know she had any elders; and the way she expressed her opinion of their weaknesses actually carried their feelings for her clear over the point of exaspiration into the region of perpetual laughter. Mother always laughed when she spoke of her, but there was an expression of perplexity in the laugh, as any one could see.

Mother never seemed to try to establish any authority over little aunt Mary; and I do believe that there was something in the sphere of the child's thought that prevented it. She was a queenly child. She was utterly unconscious of her own ignorance, and entirely loyal to some secret sense of self-respect. She was not a pretty child, though she thought she was; and she grew into one of the most beautiful women that ever was seen. She was never insolent, and was too fearless to lie, or even to equivocate; but she held her own against my mother's sneers and accusations of vanity by the frankest avowals, and sustained her avowals by such argument as her childish brain could suggest, and I never saw her angry in my life. She reigned—a veritable empress—among us children, of whom there were several by this time, and more coming. We were actual servants for her. She did what she pleased with us, and we were proud to be considered worthy of waiting on her, and of receiving her protection in return. For she did, indeed, protect us. If mother perceived the least particle of vanity cropping out in one of us, she nipped it in the bud instantly. And I can remember how little aunt Mary could don her queenly manner on such occasions, and with a face perfectly free from fear would say, for instance, "Sister, why do you say that Helen has red hair? You know it is the poet's rarest golden." (She had read such stuff as this out of our fairy stories.) "And you know, sister, that Helen is a beautiful child, and the best little girl to mind *me* that there is in the family."

It made no difference what mother said after this. Aunt Mary would soon be wearing my best string of beads, leaving me destitute of ornament. Mother—who was really sweet-tempered—often laughed and called me a little dunce; but aunt Mary would again come to my defence, and prove by argument that convinced me—if no one else—that I was a child of vast intelligence.

Gus had now reached an age when he might have become unmanageable, if it had not been for little aunt Mary. Mother's stringent efforts to keep him at home and away from other boys were making him sly. He had begun to have many a stolen pleasure, and to deceive mother as much as possible. Moreover, he had roped me into his assistance in this deception, so that when he needed some one to prove an alibi for him, a small amount of training would make me entirely competent for the transaction. I was secretly afraid to tell a lie, for I had a wholesome dread of the punishment attached to such transgressions, namely, that the liar "has his part in the lake that burneth with brimstone forever," but that seemed a good way off, whereas Gus's whipping was a sure thing and very close at hand. Then, too, I was very young, and Gus had promised me faithfully a hundred times that if I died and went to the "bad place" that he would go there with me and whip the devil and all his imps, and bring me home again.

The supreme trust little girls have in their older brothers is almost pathetic. Gus lied to me, and I lied to mother for him with great willingness; and he spent as much time with bad boys as he pleased. But little aunt Mary changed all this. She told him that she wanted him to stay in of evenings and entertain her. She said she was a fairy queen, and had to have her subjects about her. She told him that there was no boy in all the town that would compare with him. She said she loved to look at him because he was *so pretty*.

And Gus stayed at home of evenings to give little aunt Mary a chance to admire his beauty. She made him read out loud to her and me, though he was a poor reader and hated his books like poison. But little aunt Mary was always acting a part in obedience to some secret thought of her own; a thought that placed her on some high pinnacle in authority, and rendered the presence of obedient worshipers necessary. She made use of us to the utmost extent of her power; but she would not let others do it. If ever for a moment one of us rebelled, she used argument and flattery to conquer us, and this succeeded. She was never angry, and she was never unpleasant in the exhibition of her power.

If mother reproved us, aunt Mary remonstrated. "You ought not to say such things, sister," she would say to mother, "it sounds too hard. You ought not to hurt your children's feelings. They are such good little things, and so pretty and smart."

Mother's ever ready laugh was the usual response to this kind of thing; and I really expect she was pleased to have aunt Mary praise us. At all events there was a decided effect produced; for often when some of the country people, who came to our store to trade, and remained to dine with us, would say, "What a pity your gal has got red hair, 'Lizabeth; she ain't nigh so likely as the boy." Mother would answer quite earnestly, "Her hair is not red. Can't you see for yourself that it is the pure golden of the poets?"

But still she never admitted that any of us were at all good looking except in defence, when we had been attacked.

Little aunt Mary was an artist. Though she strictly avoided doing anything useful, she always took a maternal survey of us when we were dressed for Sunday school, and gave the finishing touch to our toilets. In me she would usually adjust my bonnet so as to make a coquetish display of my curls. For Gus she would pull down the waist of his jacket, and punch the dimple in his cheek a little deeper; and so on down to the baby, who was always flattered by any attention from her. I have seen a six-months-old baby stop crying when aunt Mary entered the room, and look at her with round, inquiring eyes as if asking what it could do to oblige her. Aunt Mary was always complimentary to the baby in a grave, queenly way, but never took it in her arms, though the little thing often wished to go to her.

The fact is, this child was a queen. I remember that on one occasion she had Gus and me bring up empty dry goods boxes into one of the upper rooms, and cover them with scraps of wall paper and tinsel and bows of old ribbon for her throne, where she wore an apron hind side before for a trail, and sat in state, while we waited on her. It was on this day that we pulled the icing off of mother's big company cake, and brought it and offered it to her on our knees. It seemed to us a great act of condescension on her part to eat it; but she did eat it, though with a superb indifference that left the impression that nothing was good enough for her.

Afterwards when confronted with the theft, Gus lied with great nimbleness, and I followed suit.

Little aunt Mary was the smallest of us three children. Gus was about an inch taller than she was; I was about her height, but weighed nearly twice as much, and was usually called "Fatty." Small and delicate looking as aunt Mary was when a child, she grew into a splendidly developed woman, several inches taller than I am.

Little aunt Mary never failed to come to our assistance when we were cast down, which was quite often, as mother believed it to be her duty to take the wind out of our sails whenever she perceived any wind in them. At such times Gus, who was a sensitive child, would cry bitterly; and I, who was not sensitive, and cared very little for mother's opinion at that time, would cry in sympathy with him. Then aunt Mary would say, "Why, little folks, sister don't understand either of you. The reason she has not got a better opinion of you is because she don't know much herself. You are really lovely children. Of course you are not so pretty and smart as I am, but when you get as old as I am, you will be; that is, if you are good and mind all I tell you."

How my heart would swell with gratitude when she would say such things to us, and Gus's handsome dark eyes would be so soft and luminous that his face was angelic; for he was really one of the most beautiful boys that ever lived, and looked like an infant god in comparison with little aunt Mary; but I did not draw comparisons then. I took aunt Mary at her own valuation, and prayed every night, after my other prayer was said, to be made like her.

CHAPTER II.

"SMARTEST YOUNGUN 'AT EVER LIVED, B'GOSH."

None of us liked Sunday school. Perhaps I should have said in the first part of this sketch that I was born in Fairfield, Illinois; and, at the time of which I am writing, the town did not contain more than three hundred people. There was no church there, but an occasional preacher preached in the court house. Sunday school was also held in the court house, and aunt Sally Linthecum was the president, vice-president, superintendent and teacher.

She was not my aunt, but was called aunt Sally by everybody. She was an old maid near fifty years of age at this time. She was tall, full-muscled and strong. Her hair was very light colored, but not gray, and she was really a wonderfully handsome blond. It was with difficulty that she could read; but she was very religious, and had started the Sunday school herself. As I remember now, it seems to me that aunt

Sally had complete control of the whole town. I cannot recall that I went anywhere without seeing her; and wherever I saw her she was in command—doing something herself, and giving directions to others. She presided at marriages, births and funerals. She looked after the morals of the entire community. I do not know in what spirit her ministrations were received, but I believe she was rather regarded as a necessary evil.

At Sunday school the children—about thirty—sat on benches that were destitute of backs, and read a verse apiece in the Bible. Never knowing our lessons, Gus and I used to look along the class and count noses, and then count verses so as to discover the verse that would come to us. Then we would study it industriously and be in good shape to read it creditably when our time came, unless it had hard words in it. Whenever we came to a hard word we said, "Latin, skip it," and skipped on to the next word. As aunt Sally did not know the difference, it often happened that there were more "Latin, skip its" in the Bible lesson than anything else.

All this passed off well enough; but when the boys
began to trade marbles and to eat green apples on the
sly, there was a row. Many a time I have seen the
whole school in commotion. Some of the scholars in
trying to slip out were collared and brought back and
tied to the bench legs with strong cords fished out of
aunt Sally's pocket. Others were taken across her
lap and well spanked with her slipper. She was
spanking Gus one day when my little sister Lib and I
remonstrated. We slipped down off the high bench
and went to her, holding each other's hands in order to
strengthen our courage for the rebellion we contemplated. We were both crying. Gus was squirming
and making a noise loud enough to wreck the roof. I
raised a little paw that looked like a dimpled white
satin pin-cushion and struck aunt Sally on the knee,
putting about one mouse power in the blow. Lib
raised another small bunch of dimples and struck her
on the other knee. Aunt Sally would not have known
it if she had not seen it.

"Mean old thing," I said. "Mean old fing," said Lib.
"Sass me, will ye," said aunt Sally, dropping Gus

and grabbing us. She held us both in one hand while she searched her pockets for a cord. The cord was all in use. Undaunted by this deprivation she lifted her skirts and took off a garter made of flannel listing about two yards long. She tied me to the bench with it; and then taking her other garter she tied Lib up also.

I do not remember how this escapade terminated; but really it is not an overdrawn picture of aunt Sally's Sunday school.

A year or two later we had a respectable Sunday school, conducted on regulation principles; and we were compelled to go to it. This latter school was so much more uneventful than aunt Sally's, and so much duller, with such a dearth of stolen fun, that we all looked back upon aunt Sally's school with that yearning regret one feels for a joy that has gone never to return.

I have said that I would not do any housework unless actually forced to do it. But there was one thing I would do. I took good care of the children. The child next younger than I was Lib, one of the fairest little blonds I ever saw; next to her came Lloyd, and then Ivens, then four little girls, Emma, Julia and her twin sister who died young, and last of all baby Clem. There were nine of us.

I was only a baby myself when the responsibility of the younger baby began to weigh on my mind, and I would rock the cradle by the hour without being told to do it. As the number of children increased, my cares increased. It was hardly possible to see me without a baby in my arms, and one or two others tagging after me. Even in my extreme fealty to aunt Mary they were not forgotten. I was a slave to the little things, but did not seem to know it. It was my love for them that enslaved me, rather than any compulsion from my mother. But it must have been an immense relief to her to have some one with them she could trust as she trusted me; and I have no doubt but this is the reason she was so lenient with me in the matter of dish washing and other household work.

I was rather disinclined to activity. I did not climb trees and indulge in sports that called for much exertion. I followed the other children rather as a protector than anything else. Wherever they were I was close at hand with the baby in my arms. Their childish plays amused me, and I was a great laugher; "The happiest-hearted child on earth," the neighbors used to say; but I knew it was not so. There was always the pressure of some undeveloped force in my brain, and it pushed me forward to—I did not know what. But it was forever there urging me on like an uneasy conscience; and I felt that I was loitering, and a fugitive from duty. How did I get such an idea?

I cannot remember when I learned to read. I was a great reader, though our collection of books was meager—"Pilgrim's Progress," "Fox's Book of Martyrs," that I hated and finally destroyed bit by bit on the sly. The "Arabian Nights" I read more than anything else. I read this book out loud to the children. It was a very old edition, but elaborately illustrated. We might be seen out on the grass on our stomachs with our heads in the centre of a radiating circle, ending in several pairs of feet, all of us intent upon the development of one of the startling stories.

I read these stories all the more to the children because they had power to hold them in my sight, and I was never easy if part of them were gone. I carried the responsibility of the children, I believe, much more than mother did; though probably she would have been equally as anxious about them if it had not been for her supreme trust in me.

Having my bump of ideality developed by such reading, I soon began to compose stories for them. I expect these stories were queer combinations of fairies, griffins, magicians and monsters, but they delighted the little ones. My reputation as a story teller spread through the town, and often I had dozens of eager listeners. I was greatly praised for my skill and became a centre of attraction for all the small folk of the village. After a short experience with this thing, I became ambitious and began to illustrate my tales as I told them. A pencil and a blank book were riches to me then. I could not often obtain the latter. But I had pencils enough, and I used the margins of my school books for my illustrations. Down one margin and around the bottom and up the other side my interminable caravan of "what is its" wound their way. Elephants, lions and tigers, fairies, goblins and demons were all in the procession that only ended with the last page of the book. These figures were very small, of course, but many of them were strikingly like what I intended them for. I drew them with astonishing rapidity, my tongue running on endlessly in description of the story as I continued to draw. I think there was real merit in my drawing.

I began to get a local reputation as an artist; and sometimes I ventured to take a portrait of some pretty baby, which I colored out of a ten cent paint box. I was considered a genius by the ignorant country people of whom the town was composed; and one might have thought their praise would be greatly prized by me. But for some reason or other I did not care for it. I was so intent on expressing my little ideas by tongue and pencil that I scarcely knew what people said of me. I had grown to be a very busy child in my own way. I had become self-centered—sufficient unto myself—partly from natural tendency, and partly from little aunt Mary's training that rendered me first indifferent to the adverse opinion of those about me, and afterwards rather indifferent to their good opinion.

I made no effort to attract any body's notice. I was full of my own ideas, and was always trying to work them out. At this time the pressure of that strange mental force, which had so often seemed to be driving me, was less. It was outflowing in congenial expression; it was partly appeased. I was becoming more free; less pent up in my organism.

But though I made no effort to attract attention, and was happier with my drawing materials on the floor, and the baby seated near, than when surrounded by crowds of admiring urchins, yet I was the attracting centre on all occasions. Children abandoned their play to congregate around me and see and hear what I was saying and doing. I did not need nor want them, but they came. I have since discovered the law in this matter. Intentness of purpose concentrates the faculties of a person. Such a person becomes a magnet. Knowing this, anyone can become a magnet through the practice of concentration. This power is developed through the study of Mental Science. I seemed to have it naturally when a child. Later in life I think I lost it; but now, with the knowledge of how to regain it, it is coming back in great force.

Self-centered children are more or less indifferent to praise and blame. Among my own children there was one who was wonderfully self-centered. Lying on the floor, with her fat legs turned up over her back, molding pigs and horses out of the inside of an underbaked biscuit, it was impossible to attract her attention from her work. She was so sweet and fair, and so entirely independent, that she drew our hearts most powerfully. To pick her up and half smother her with kisses was a temptation that some of us could not resist.

"Top it! top it! Do way, put me down; me 'pises to be tissed; now don't oo do it adin." Such remarks as these were the only return we got for our love. And this child, whose greatest wish was to be let alone, was followed and watched with deep interest by all the other children near. She was self-centered. She drew to herself all those who were less self-centered than she was. She was always busy, always working out some idea of her own.

I wonder if anyone is interested in this "Meandering Mike" of a narrative. I stop writing occasionally to ask this question; and then I find myself smiling as I recall some episode of child character that once passed under my observation, perhaps a long time ago. For I have always been a close observer of children, and I have had more good laughs at the little darlings than at all other things in life put together. I could fill a book with their absurdities, their charming characteristics and their quaint oddities, and sometimes I have thought I would do it.

Up to the age of perhaps nine or ten years I had very little respect for what was called the truth. I am sure that I weighed matters in my mind and came to the conclusion that lying was not only easier, but more comfortable all round than seeing the children whipped, or even scolded or punished. I had to choose between two disagreeable alternatives, and I chose that which best suited my feelings. It is true that I frequently wabbled a little in my choice when mother held the fear of hell fire before my eyes, but this fear had not taken a deep hold on me then, though it did so later.

I remember on one occasion that she held out a strong incentive to me to tell the truth. She said that if I confessed a lie after I had told it God would forgive me, and that I would be saved. This set me to thinking, and I concluded that my best plan was to lie first and confess afterwards, and so save my own soul as well as my brother's body.

It must be remembered that up to this time I really was not much afraid of the "bad place," because I was quite sure that Gus could wipe it out, root and branch, before it could hurt me. And yet I could see that there might be an easier way of dodging it, and mother's suggestion appealed to me as decidedly business like; so I tried it a short time afterwards.

One day I had been drawing the "long bow" more than usual. Everything had gone wrong with the children, and mother had the headache so that her nerves were unstrung. I never remember a day when she took down the rawhide from its nail so often. I was almost wild and lied right and left recklessly.

That night I was awakened by a terrific storm of thunder and lightning. It filled me with fear, and made all previous descriptions of the "bad place" a terrible reality. I began to think that I needed forgiveness very much indeed. I slipped out of bed and went into mother's room.

"Mother," I said, "I have been telling a great many stories, and I want to confess them."

"Tell me all about them," said mother.

Then she waited, and I waited. "Well, go on," said mother.

I had not thought what to tell her, and now that I did think, I could recall nothing that would not involve some of the children. I was sure this would not do.

"Go on, Helen," said mother.

I knew in a moment that I must trust my wits; so I said: "When you told me the other day that I should not go blackberrying with the children, I went, and then told you that I did not go."

"I can't remember that I told you not to go. What day was it?"

"Oh! one day not long ago."

"Not long ago? Why, I am sure I am always glad when you take them away and keep them from bothering me. What day was it?"

"Oh! not long ago; just the other day. Oh! yes, it was last summer, or summer before last; I remember now."

"Very well," said mother, "you are a good little girl to confess it, and God will forgive you."

This was encouraging. It raised my spirits and limbered up my imagination to its work, so that I composed another lie, and told it with great glibness. She praised me again. Then I told her another, and several others. In the flashes of lightning I could see the bright eyed baby sitting up in bed watching me, and listening. I had waked him up. I could see mother's interested face high up on the pillow, but father's face I could not see. I hoped he was asleep. He was a man of irrepressible humor, and I felt uneasy about his hearing my confessions. As these confessions proceeded there came at last the gurgling sound of laughter that could no longer be suppressed. "Send her to bed, Lib," said father; "don't you know the little monkey is making that up as she goes along?"

"Oh!" I cried, "I am afraid to go to bed for fear the devil will get me."

Then he got up and took me by the hand. "Will the devil get me?" I asked.

"Damn the devil," he said.

Mother groaned. I was horrified. It was the first time I had ever heard him swear. And then to think he had sworn about so influential a character as the devil was too awful. I expected the floor to open and swallow us all up. I screamed hysterically.

He took me in his arms soothingly and carried me up stairs and slept with me until morning.

It is astonishing that the majority of parents know so little of the power of terror over the minds of their children. A child's imagination is so strong and masterful that it needs only a suggestion of something frightful to fire it to the verge of insanity. Nobody knows what sufferings the little ones undergo from this one source. There is no offense for which I would discharge a nurse or attendant so promptly as for an attempt to frighten a child.

That night before I fell asleep my father told me there was no devil and no hell; but his words had little effect upon me in comparison with mother's fixed conviction. I knew that my father often spoke impulsively, and that mother treated many of his assertions with marked incredulity; so I took sides with her because her faith expressed my own fears, and I was afraid not to fear. And yet it was not until I was some years older that this horrid doctrine began to poison my mind in a way that almost wrecked my reason.

Little aunt Mary was away from us a great deal at the time I began to have such power as an entertainer of the other children; and when she was with us for short visits she took no interest in my work. Her indifference to it acted like a rebuke upon me, which I certainly felt to a degree that shook my interest in it without entirely causing me to abandon it.

It must be acknowledged that my fealty to little Aunt Mary was also rather marred for a time, though I really never outgrew it. I was drawn in two opposite directions at once, and the result was a standstill. Her visits at this time were interruptions in the steady unfoldment of my own individuality, and as they became more frequent they marred it to a great extent. I began to be part aunt Mary and part myself. In this half-and-half condition I became more open to the opinions of those about me.

I think now, as I compare my character during childhood with that of the children I am acquainted with to-day, that I was more independent of popular opinion than the majority. There was an immense amount of "push" about me, which though pretty well concealed—for I dared not make much display of it—indicated a strength of individualism that was never—through the whole course of my after life—totally crushed. Indeed, it was never crushed in the least. It was "side-tracked" over and over again for short intervals, but during these intervals I really believe it was gathering force rather than losing it.

It is a fact that children who have this force of individualism are always more indifferent to the opinions of others than children of weaker will. It is this latter class who are more easily managed than any others, by working on their love of approbation.

My parents had no such hold on me. Praise did not stimulate me to effort nor did blame. It was evident that I had something unseen towards which I was working, the attracting power of which overbalanced the considerations that ordinarily serve as a stimulus to many children. I did not know what it was myself any more than the bulb knows of the lily folded within its layers; but I felt the developing force, and was in a great measure obedient to it. I would have my own way; I pushed past obstacles; I climbed over them or crept under them; any direction that presented the least resistance in the attainment of my wish was the direction I took. I could not get my own way openly and by telling the truth, but I usually gained it "by ways that are dark and tricks that are vain," like Bret Harte's "Heathen Chinee."

Now if my inclinations had been bad I should have given my parents great trouble; for I belonged to that class of youngsters called "headstrong." But my natural inclinations all ran towards harmony and peace, and the development of the beautiful, and the love and protection of children and helpless things; and every bit of lying I ever did was prompted by a perfectly enormous mother love, and a sympathy as wide as the world; a love and sympathy so great as to make truth telling entirely subordinate to my desire to protect all creatures from suffering. I think my mother had a half way idea of this, for she did not correct me much or severely. And after she was dead—she died suddenly when I was only a young girl—a letter was found that she had written the day before to one of her sisters in which she said: "While all my children have been good and lovely, and have blest me most abundantly, I think perhaps that Helen, with her devotion to her sisters and brothers and her generous nature, has been the greatest help of all."

And yet Gus was her favorite. She was so proud of him, and he was so handsome and manly I cannot wonder at it. Then I always believed that Lib stood next in her affections. Lib was such a fair, dainty little thing; so tender and yielding and dependent, and so extraordinarily pretty. She looked like mother, too, and it sometimes happens that this fact tightens the link between mother and daughter.

Not having much time to be sensitive, with so many ideas of my own to work out, I gave small heed to the thought of being sandwiched between these two beautiful children. There never was a brat more light-hearted and free from jealousy than I was. I gloried in the charms of the others without thinking much about myself in any way. I must have been a good-looking child, however, in spite of being too fat—which was considered a great drawback to my appearance. I was so healthy! In all my experience I have never seen any one so impervious to disease. The place in which we lived was very sickly. It was the Wabash bottom lands. The town had timber on one side and prairie on the other, and the location was really very pretty to look at. But such another hole for every form of disease I surely never heard of. This was many years ago, and these conditions are now changed. But then every head there was full of beliefs in disease, and in its power as an active factor in human concerns. It was God-appointed; and when death resulted it was God's judgment. Nevertheless, in spite of God and his judgment, the main business of the inhabitants was paying doctors in the hope of annulling the effort of Almighty wisdom in exterminating them.

It not unfrequently happened that three-fourths of every family in town was bedfast at one time. In the spring it was spring fever; in the fall it was winter fever; in the summer it was "milk sickness"; and all the time it was "fever 'n' ager." It was said of that town that the court house bell was rung three times a day for the inhabitants to take quinine. Truly there were plenty of little children whose abdomens were so distended with enlarged spleens, and whose limbs were so shrunken that they looked like very young frogs just emerged from the tadpole condition. Many of the people were so poor that the children only wore one garment in warm weather, and it so short and narrow that it did not conceal the shape of the distorted little bodies. It goes without saying that most of them died in childhood, and that funerals were so common as to make no impression on my mind at all.

All of our children had turns of being sick except me, and it was a great trial to me that I was so overlooked. I longed to have only one chill and fever, if more were denied me. But hope and pray as I would I could not get sick. My skin was as fair as the petals of a blush rose, and my hair hung in massive waves and curls, and had the healthy luster and the bright color of well pulled molasses candy. I was as fat as a "butterball" duck; and wherever there was the proper place for a bone to protrude, as in knees and elbows and knuckle joints, in me there were nothing but dimples.

Once I pretended to be sick, and mother gave me a dose of calomel, rhubarb and jalap, with occasional tea cups full of senna tea that came very near killing me. The last dose she brought was too much for my patience. I flung myself about and finally got out behind the bed and sat on the floor howling. Mother could not reach me, but she sent my little brother Lloyd to me with the nauseating dose in his hands. The little fellow begged me to take it, and when I would not, he drank it himself saying he "spected" it would do as much good, and mother would not know the difference. My ardent desire to be sick was now cooled; but I was very proud of the experience, because it seemed to give me an entrance into the grand social privilege of the place; that of talking about the time when I had "the fever and came mighty nigh dyin'."

It is difficult to realize the amount of medicine that was taken in those days. The neighbors had a way of keeping the empty bottles to show to each other; and I think it was a matter of rivalry among them to see which one had the greatest number. I have an idea that there was some claim to moral or intellectual superiority attached to the matter. I am sure that when this subject was under discussion, and this was as often as a group of them chanced to meet, I felt disreputably small and out of fashion because I had no claims to distinction based on the number of medicine bottles I had emptied.

I cannot say, however, that it rankled in my mind, nor do I hold it responsible for a little episode I am about to relate. Mother believed in medicine, not only as a curative for present ills, but as a preventive for expected ones. So when the weather seemed to be warm, or cool, or medium, or very cold, or when indications prophesied any of these conditions, she thought it best for us to take a dose of quinine every morning before breakfast; and I being the proper person was always appointed to administer it. The quinine was in liquid form and was given with a teaspoon. The children hated it, and it was all I could do to get them to take it. But I believed in its efficacy to such an extent that I thought their lives depended on it. Of course this lent such power to my efforts that not one of them ever escaped.

It was mother's understanding that I was to take it too; and the one grain of consolation to the poor little ones was that my turn would come. So when they were through I would pour my own tea-spoonfull and raise it to my lips, and turn and run to the corner of the porch where the honeysuckle vine was so thick, and where I could dispose of it without detection. Then coming back I would meet them with a face as expressive of a bad taste as their own. There were other ways of eluding their vigilance when this one wore out; but my character suffered a good deal from the doubts that were reflected on my veracity, and I had to do something desperate to switch public opinion off the track. So one morning I took the bottle, a large one, and quite full, and gave the children to understand that I would satisfy them; and I drank the contents down, every drop of it, in full view of the entire group.

They were breathless for a moment and then ran, panic stricken, to mother. Poor mother was awfully frightened and sent for our family physician. He was a doctor of home-made manufacture, and had never seen the inside of a college in his life; but he was really one of the most successful practitioners I ever saw; and this was because he was so vital, so high spirited and so jolly. His laugh could be heard half a mile away, and it was more efficacious than his medicine.

When the doctor came I was on the lounge, and he approached me rapidly and with the gravest face I had ever seen him wear. His expression was such that for a moment I was psychologized into forgetting that I had cautiously emptied the quinine out of the bottle an hour before and filled it up with water. I began to think maybe I would die, and a cold sweat started on me as he felt my pulse and examined my tongue and placed his hand on my heart, etc.

For two long hours they watched for symptoms.

Breakfast came and was eaten, and I not there. Mercy, how hungry I was! I had not calculated on so serious a deprivation.

The doctor grew suspicious and attempted to cross-question me, but I declined to commit myself. At last he prepared to leave. "Is there any particular diet I shall give her?" asked mother.

"Oh! yes, Lib," said he as he stood with the door knob in his hand, "be very careful of her diet; don't give her anything more indigestible than india rubber flap jacks and hard boiled goose eggs."

Years after this, seated in a handsome carriage behind a spanking Kentucky team with this same doctor, then a widower for the second time, but still a strikingly handsome man, though verging toward sixty, he made me an offer of marriage which I declined. Afterwards, to fill an embarrassing interval that ensued, I told him how I had deceived everybody about the quinine.

"Smartest young un 'at ever lived, b'gosh," said the doctor cheerfully; "roped me in then, and have roped me in again when I am old enough to know better. B'gosh! I don't know what to do with you."

CHAPTER III.

A LOVE LETTER.

The previous chapter is far from giving an adequate idea of my experience with sickness. Owing to the natural motherhood of me, I became a splendid nurse even when quite young.

I had to take my turn sitting up of nights with our own sick children, and as it often happened in the morning after one of my nights that the little patient was better, it came to be believed that I had some special and heaven-endowed gift of healing.

In those days the practice of medicine was very rigid. No matter how high the patient's fever ran, all water was forbidden. Certain diet was prescribed with the death penalty attached to a deviation from it. No fruit was allowed; no acids of any kind; and the most powerful medicines were given at fixed intervals. I recall the very first night from which my reputation as a nurse took its rise. My little sister Emma, just nine years younger than I, was subject to bilious attacks in which she was almost consumed with fever. She was the sweetest child, and the most angelically beautiful one, in the world, I thought. She was the special pet of the entire family and of the whole town. She was called the flower of mother's flock on account of the loveliness of her disposition, never manifesting a particle of ill-temper on any occasion; always obliging, happy-hearted and generous. This darling sister is still living—a very beautiful woman yet—beloved by all who know her.

On the night referred to, mother had no sooner gone to bed leaving me alone with the little sick creature, then only three years old, than she began to beg for water. Her large, pleading, innocent eyes would not release mine for an instant, and her coaxing little voice tore my heart in pieces. "Oh! Henny, watty, watty, please; please, dear Henny."

I begged and plead with her. My tears answered her moans, for her parched eyeballs were moistureless. When I could hold out no longer I gave her just one swallow, and watched its effects. She kept begging for more, and I gave it. Before an hour I took a tumbler out on the back porch where the well stood, and brought her a whole glass, cool and dripping. Oh! how she drank it. Then I gave her another and another. I knew symptoms well enough to see that she was getting no worse; and presently her pulse went down, and she slept while the perspiration came out on her forehead. I do not know that I ever passed a night in such terror; but her sleep was so healthful and her skin so natural, that I became reassured and began to do some thinking for myself; especially as she woke up hungry as a hunter just before day, and begged for some bread and butter and jam. These were forbidden things too; but one act of boldness prepares the faltering soul for another, and I gave her what she wanted, carefully clearing away all signs of my disobedience and making her promise never to tell. When mother came in Emma was asleep again, and before the new day passed she was virtually well.

Cause and effect are largely developed in my head. I learned my lesson from this night's experience, and every patient that I attended reaped the benefit of it. And this is why I got the reputation of being a heaven-ordained healer. This, and another thing equally as important, that of throwing the medicine away. The children hated to take it, and after a few cautious experiments in throwing part of it away I got to throwing it all away.

I expect the reader will wonder that a naturally bold, frank child should do all this in an underhanded manner. I find in looking back at myself that in spite of my boldness and frankness I was secretive. I cannot tell what argument passed through my immature brain, but I suppose I knew that the opposition was too strong for me, and that I could only have my own way by taking it on the sly; and it is my opinion now that it took a very daring child to do as I did, even though I did it with such extreme caution.

And no doubt I had some system of reasoning that justified me to myself. I think all children have. And because this is so, I beg every mother in the world to use patience and argument with her little ones, and abstain forever from the brutality of a blow. If parents will conquer themselves they will find that they will not need to conquer their children. The silent and peaceful breath of self-conquest communicates itself without even a spoken word, and harmonizes every discordant element in the family.

Now, will it be believed, that somehow or other this knowledge was in me when I was a child, and all my secrecy and deceptions were in the line of its unfoldment under such difficulties as I necessarily met in the organized opinions of that time?

It was too big an undertaking—in the face of so much opposition—to explain myself; and probably I was quite unable to do it, even if I had wished to; so I simply pushed forward in the accomplishment of what seemed most desirable, working silently in lines that presented the fewest obstacles.

I find this same disposition with me still. I never argue with anyone. People may argue with me, but they will have it all to themselves. They may think they have convinced me, and yet they have not swerved me by the tenth part of the frailest idea. It is the same way about giving advice. I never do it; and it is useless for any one to offer it to me. There is some unseen goal to which every attribute of my whole nature is true as the needle to the pole; and it always was. That this leading is in the line of my individual development, I do not doubt. To me it means life itself, and the abandonment of it would be the abandonment of life.

The chief difference I find between myself as I then was, and myself as I now am, lies in the fact that while I was formerly secretive and obtained my own way by deception, if I could not have it otherwise, that now I am bold enough to scorn deception, and I value the trend of my individual unfoldment too highly to care a straw for the opinions of other people regarding it. I take my own course openly, and pursue it earnestly. If friends approve I am glad; if they oppose I bear their opposition stoically; but in any case I keep straight on; nothing swerves me.

And what does this mean? I believe it means simply *fidelity to my own individual self-hood;* fidelity to that consciousness which distinguishes me from the consciousness of another: fidelity to my own sense of what is best, in distinction from the sense of another as to what is best.

We sometimes speak of a child as a natural-born liar. There are no natural-born liars. Take off the pressure that would warp a child out of the line of its own individual and original development, and that child immediately becomes truthful. It is an ignorant system of bringing children up that makes them lie. It is a condition of irresolution fostered in them by making them afraid to have their own way, even when every current of their being is set upon doing so. In such a case the child is open to choose either his own suppression or a suppression of the truth. If he is a weak child he consents to be suppressed, and becomes what his parents call a truthful child, but with a broken will. If he is a strong, vital, headstrong child, he will have his own way and lie about it. But when these children are grown up, it is the latter type that make the world movers, and the former type that make the hangers on.

And again I object to the term truthful as applied to the first class, and to the word liar as applied to the second class. For I say that fidelity to one's self, to one's most earnest desires, is a truthfulness that stands far above that trained infidelity to self, which involves the surrender of the will for the sake of being considered a good boy or girl.

So far as my deceptions were concerned, I was perfectly free from self-accusation during my childhood. I was conscious of something that justified me. Farther on I got a definition of the situation that satisfied me up to the time my reason became submerged by the fear which the plan of salvation engendered in my mind. After that I had no ideas of my own about anything for years.

But my definition of a lie was this. If a thing was said with an intent to harm another person, that thing was a lie, no matter how true it was; but if it was said in the interest of peace and harmony and happiness, it was true even though every word was false. I was very far from telling this to mother, or, indeed, as a rule to any one, but once when my father and I became confidential I told him, and he said I was the most truthful little girl he ever saw. I would have trusted my father with all my thoughts but for a certain expression in his laughing eyes that made me think he was making fun of me. As it was I lived two lives. One, the unseen one, was purely ideal, and everything was beautiful there. The other was my external, every-day life that I tried to conform to the ideal one. Actually I carried a heaven about with me into which all my friends were admitted without their knowing it; and while there they were all perfect. Not one of them had any deficiency of person or character, and they were all rich and dressed in silk and satin and lace every day. Not a soul of my acquaintance was excluded except for a little while at a time; as, for instance, some child that had slapped one of our children, or otherwise offended my sense of right.

Among these friends who lived in this secret heaven were people who were to all intents and purposes entirely unfit for any heaven whatever. They were the riffraff of one of the most ignorant communities in the United States. But I brought them in and dressed them up and made them good and happy.

There were three little girls whose mother was very poor, and a dreadful woman besides. These little things would come trailing into school of a morning, the eldest in front and the others following Indian file. The town boys called them Rag, Tag and Bobtail, and treated them badly. I made no effort to defend them; I reproved no child for his cruelty; I simply could not do it at that tender age; but when alone I took these little girls into my Paradise and made princesses of them, and gave them higher places of honor than any of their persecutors.

I had quite a struggle with myself to admit boys at all, except my brothers. I did not like boys. The expression I most frequently used in describing them was that "they had no sense."

How they could find their chief pleasure in torturing things I could not understand, and in fighting each other. It was such a mystery to me that I actually thought them deficient in mental capacity. I was afraid of them, and would go a good way out of my road rather than meet one if I was alone. But we had a girl in school who was not afraid, and did I not glory in her pluck?

The school was taught in an upper room in the court house. In dismissing it, the teacher always sent the boys out first. When they reached the outer door—instead of leaving, as was expected of them—they often stopped and formed two lines through which the girls had to pass. As we passed out, they would jeer and taunt those among us against whom they had a grudge. The girl to whom I have just alluded was certainly a peculiar specimen of humanity. She had the features and carriage of a Greek goddess; but her beauty was marred by a perpetual frown. The whole world went wrong with her, and her position towards it was bitterly antagonistic. Such a fighter as she was! Her father, who died early, was an Irishman, and a truly grand character. Her mother was the softest, most baby-like, pretty little bit of a woman I ever saw, but slightly deaf. She was married again to a man younger than herself; and all the horrors relating to the cruelty of step-fathers were far outdone by the cruelty practiced on him by his step-children, of whom there were three, Kate being the eldest and the leader. It seems surprising to me now to recall her boldness and courage. We more timid girls would pass down between the two lines of boys, and take a safe position where we would wait for Kate. I can see her now as she suddenly appeared in the door on such occasions, her form erect and divinely muscular; her features so perfect that her freckles hardly had power to mar her beauty; her blue eyes covert, almost downcast, but emitting baleful gleams from under the drooping lids; bareheaded, too, with her slat sunbonnet clubbed in her stout right hand. In those days our sunbonnets were filled with hickory splints, and could be converted into quite formidable weapons. And there I seem to see her standing, without a word, as the boys dare her to come on, distorting their faces with diabolical grimaces and writhing their bodies into such shapes as appear most threatening and dangerous. Kate waits her opportunity, knowing that such unusual movements as they are making in their effort to terrorize her, will exhaust their muscles. Finally when she is ready she springs from the door step upon them with the agility of a tiger, and knocks two or three down just by the sheer force of her flying form; clips a half dozen more on the head with her clubbed bonnet; digs her claws into another, kicks three or four more, butts another with her head and makes his nose bleed; and keeps this up until she puts them all to rout, or at least banishes them so far that they content themselves with throwing stones at her in the intervals of nursing their bruises. But she herself is an adept at throwing stones, having served an apprenticeship on her step-father, and they have no advantage of her in this matter.

I loved this girl, and we grew up close friends. She was intellectual and developed a taste for reading. She made a splendid woman and a social leader. She married and was the mother of extraordinarily fine children. After thirty years absence from the town I went back there to find her insane. Her strength, her force, the very majesty of her intellect, having found no outlet suitable to their grand character, had turned to rend her. A few years later she died.

Next to me, in respect to age, was my sister Lib, named after mother; then there were two boys, Lloyd and Ivens. These two little villains gave me more trouble than all the rest of the children. Wherever one went the other went, and what mischief one could not suggest, the other could. They stuck together like a pair of pickpockets, and never were known to turn state's evidence against each other, no matter what the provocation. I was eternally carrying these youngsters out of danger; and as they were large, heavy children, the best I could do was to take them around the body below their arms and drag them away. In doing this they had the free use of their feet; and I am not exaggerating when I say that there were years that I was never once free from bruises from my knees to my ankles, inflicted by them. Now, while I really loved them, they never seemed to me like Gus. Gus was the man of the house; but these little unkempt cubs were a pair of troglodytes that by careful preservation from death, might develop into second editions of my beautiful elder brother. This was the way I felt towards them, and my care of them was unflagging; and I do really suppose that a great part of it was unnecessary.

The fence that bounded the back part of our garden was made of boards, with one flat board on the top that—on Saturdays—served as a seat for us children. Just across the street was a saloon where intoxicating drinks were served, and where on this particular day of the week, half the men in the county were collected to talk, drink and have a social time. All along this street were hitching posts erected, and many horses were tied to them. Indeed, the town was full of horses and men on this day. It seemed as if everybody—by common consent—dropped work and came to town on Saturday. It was like a circus to us; and we were in the habit of sitting on the fence patiently from morning until evening—unless the men got to shooting each other—and entering into the excitement of the occasion. What drunken brawls we witnessed, and what horse racing and big talk and threats, all of it usually winding up in a half dozen harmless fights! It was only very rarely that any one had a pistol to use.

Now, will some one tell me how it was that with my naturally peaceful disposition I entered into the riotous enjoyment of these wild scenes? For I surely did enjoy them. Then, too, I had no trouble with the children on these days. They sat there with me in perfect content; even the baby would be quiet and happy as it watched the busy panorama and listened to the neighing, screaming horses. It must have been *the life in it* that was so attractive. It was in such vivid contrast with the other days of the week, whose monotonous, droning events were only one remove from death.

At least I would think so now if I had to live that life over again, having known something better; but then I did not really feel its dullness. I was too superbly alive myself not to see life in everything. Fat and lazy as I was, and nearly always loaded down with the weight of a baby, yet I was the most interested spectator of the doings of the ants and bees and other small folk of the fields, which I would follow with great interest to their homes and do what I could to discover their habits without hurting them. And I was interested in the people about me. I knew when Mary Ellen Watkins, aunt Emma's hired girl, would have money enough saved up to buy a pink calico dress and a pair of prunello slippers; I kept accounts for her. The wages of a hired girl in those days, and in that place, were fifty cents a week. Other things were proportionally, cheap. Think of hens that had no more spirit than to supply the market with eggs at three cents a dozen; but they actually did it. The "new hen" in this Bloomer stage of female development values her services more highly.

Those were primitive times. I cannot recall the unseen working of the system of industry that prevailed, but I know that the women spun and wove flax and wool, and made the material they and their families used for clothing. Where they got the flax I do not know. I know where they got wool, because every family kept a few sheep. Every neighborhood had its own shoemaker who got enough work to do to support him. The shoes he made were simply dreadful to behold. But ugly as they were, the best of care was taken by his customers to make them last as long as possible. I have met many a crowd of people, young and old, coming home from church carrying their shoes in their hands to save the wear of walking in them.

My condition in life differed quite materially from that of many of the people about me. My father "kept store." We did not wear homespun clothes nor home-made shoes. We were called "quality folks," to indicate this fact, and were greatly looked to by many of our neighbors, and especially by the country people.

Mother was decidedly a society leader. To our Fairfield swelldom she was what the Four Hundred are to New York; or what the immortal Worth was to Paris, and indeed to all the world. Mother found out some how or other that little girls wore drawers, and made some for me. I remember her trying the first pair on me. She had me stripped and standing in the middle of the room. It must have been cold weather for there was a fire. I also recall the fact that aunt Clem and aunt Emma were present. Aunt Emma had too much sympathy with children to laugh, but aunt Clem roared, and mother could not keep her face straight, though she tried.

"Sister," said aunt Clem, "she is the living image of old Johnny Young." And then they fairly whooped.

Johnny Young came to town every Saturday during warm weather, dressed in tow linen trousers and shirt, with knit "galluses." He weighed four hundred pounds, and was a sight to behold. One of aunt Clem's little girls was caught stalking him in the street one day, tiptoeing after him like a hunter after his game. In describing him she said, "He was awfy behind, but he was *awfy* before."

To be compared with old Johnny was an insult I could not stand. I became sulky and would not move except as I was pushed around. When they were done, and had taken the drawers off, I picked them up and ran and threw them in the fire. What followed I do not remember. As I was in good spanking costume I probably got spanked; but if so, a spanking was such a slight insult in comparison with being said to resemble Johnny Young, I have forgotten it.

The drawers, however, became an established institution, and my dresses, which had formerly been down to my shoe tops were shortened almost to my knees. The drawers came clear to my feet; and my appearance may be imagined. One day as I was passing the store, a man from the country, a regular "Blue Jeans"—that was what we town people called them—spoke to me. He said, "I don't know whether to call you Sis or Bub; but I want to say that *my* boys wear breeches, but my gals don't."

I said nothing. I was too timid, too startled; but I held that man in profound contempt for years, and rarely a day passed that I did not—in imagination—make some elaborately cutting reply to his remark. I was then, and am still, troubled with "after wit."

But, my mother being a great social leader, it was not long until all the respectable families in town had drawers on their little girls; or, if not drawers, then an imitation of them in the form of "pantalets." These peculiar garments were bags in which the lower part of the leg was incased. They were tied below the knee with the same string that held the stocking up. One disrespectful boy in town called them "shin curtains," and remarked sneeringly that if people were as modest as they ought to be, they would put them on the bedstead legs too—for all of which his ears must have burned fearfully, if there is anything in signs, for we little girls did cat-haul him unmercifully behind his back; and finally, as the most withering piece of sarcasm, and the most irredeemable reproach, we changed his name from Fay Turney to "Fraternity." This, to our infantile intelligences, seemed such a stroke of sarcasm that, out of pure self-gratulation, we forgave him. Later, but while still children, I was the recipient of Fay's youthful affections, and got a love letter from him. He gave one of my little brothers a goose egg to bring it to me. Goose eggs were legal tender there, and the Goose folk in the neighborhood of town must have had a difficult time to increase their families owing to the depredations of the boys.

I did not like Fay's letter because it alluded to points concerning which I had a right to be sensitive, having already heard too much about them. He said that "some folks didn't like fat girls, but he did; and some folks didn't like red hair, but he did; Hall Wilson said I looked like I was cut out of a solid piece of salt junk, and he meant to taste of me some time and find out; but he, Fay, had lain in wait at a certain fence corner and flung a stick at Hall that mighty nigh split his fool noodle plum open." This and more like it went to make up Fay's letter, which I would not have considered a love letter but for his emphatic assertion of the fact, and by his winding up with some poetry that everybody in town would have sworn was indelible proof:

"The rose is red, the violet's blue,
Sugar's sweet, and so are you."

The next time I met Fay on the street, I picked up a pebble and held it tight in my hand until I had passed him without looking at him. When a safe distance behind him, I threw it at him wickedly, and ran as fast as I could.

Fay passed from the world of sense years and years ago; and Hall Wilson, who was going to find out by a practical test whether I was cut out of salt junk or not, got to be private secretary to President Lincoln. It was not long after Lincoln's death before Hall—still young, handsome and talented—joined the silent majority. What a strange feeling of stillness comes over me when I think of all these old companions so long gone.

CHAPTER IV.

THE GOODEST LITTLE BOY THAT EVER LIVED.

My two little brothers often talked of going to see the world. I discovered that the world they intended to visit was on the other side of the dimly outlined timber, just beyond the prairie, which bounded the town on the north. Several times I caught them stealing off in that direction, and dragged them back by main force. But once they got so far ahead of me I could not catch them. So I followed them, begging them to return, alternately scolding and crying. I can still see Lloyd trudging ahead sturdily, and that fat pudge of small imp, Ivens, trotting after him. It was evening and would soon be dark. My distress was simply indescribable. I was afraid of the tall grass in the prairie, which was higher than our heads, and the cow path we were in was dim and undefined. Night closed around us. We could barely distinguish the path; and yet that infant demon in the lead walked on as if made of the finest steel springs. After a long time Ivens began to lag; then I took him by the hand and still followed. Presently he began to bawl, and I tried to carry him. In this way I fell quite a distance behind Lloyd, who never once turned his head to see whether I was there or not, but marched straight on with unabated zeal. I hurried all I could to catch up with him, and the last I saw of him he was crossing a ravine on a rail or slender log placed there as a sort of primitive bridge for foot passengers. I cried out to him to stop. I was exhausted and almost breathless. It never was in me to walk a log like that, or even to "coon it." It was all I could do to navigate my tub of a craft on solid ground. As the boy went steadily over that frail crossing and disappeared in the total darkness on the other side, it was as if my life went with him. It must be remembered that in spite of my being a head-strong child, I had been frightened so much I was timid; so it is not surprising that the pictures I drew of snakes and lizards and wild cats were enough to keep me wide awake and in agony for hours, as I sat there in the dew-damp grass with Ivens in my lap, wrapped up in the short skirt of my dress to protect him from the chill of the night. He had been hungry, and had cried himself to sleep. Hours passed that seemed like ages to me. At last I heard the report of a gun, and then another and another. I knew what that meant, and rolled the fat lump of a boy out of my arms and stood up, but so stiff I could scarcely move. I heard a horse coming, and voices calling; and then every bit of vocal capacity in me limbered to the occasion, and I yelled loud enough to raise the dead. I have always had a most powerful voice.

One man took Ivens on a horse with him, and another took me. A number of men continued the search for Lloyd. They found him several miles beyond where I was sitting. He had reached the "world," and was struggling along among the trees. They brought him home by sheer force, for he was still resolved to go on. For the first time in my life I was glad to see a child whipped. But it did no good; the boy had a mania for running off, and more than once plunged us all in distress by his capers.

Lloyd was a peculiar child in more ways than one. I never understood him, and I was not at all able to manage him. He was fleet-footed as a greyhound, and strong as a young lion. He upset all authority, and carried Ivens along with him in his reckless behavior. I never knew what real trouble was until I came to have these two boys to look after. It is true that Gus was a source of perplexity, and occasionally he frightened me by some of his capers; but he was always gentle and kind and sensible, while these two boys were inconsiderate and restless, and as indifferent to consequences as a couple of Newfoundland pups. For Ivens' offenses to me, he has been overtaken by regular preacher's retribution. He married young, and has had seven boys in one unbroken line; and may the Lord have mercy on his soul. Gus, on the other hand, has a houseful of pretty daughters, and does not need mercy from any supernatural source.

Occasionally, however, Gus frightened Lib and me, but never "with malice aforethought or prepense" (if the lawyers will pardon me for quoting one of the absurdities of their vernacular).

Our family were what were called, in those times of great simplicity, high livers. That is, we had meat three times a day, and wheat bread, and plenty of preserves and other sweets. Mother was a woman of ideas. If she had lived in the reign of fads that besets the nation at this time, I cannot imagine where she would have found a stopping place. But in her time, fads were few and far between; and they were also very weak and unobtrusive little things; but they were the progenitors of all we have now, and of a thousand more not yet ushered in. But the fads of that day—such as they were—must have appealed to my mother's prophetic soul, since never one of them put its nose in our mental atmosphere that she did not lasso and harness to the chariot of her progressive ideas. So when there began to be talk about hygiene and bathing and dieting, it actually seemed as if we were to be drowned first and starved afterwards. We were permitted to eat everything the family ate except at supper, when we were provided with mush and milk and put to bed before dark. This was terrible. At least it seemed so to us. Children are very sensitive to such things. I remember that my days were clouded with gloom just because of this new edict; if the sun had gone out it would hardly have made my heart heavier.

And never a protest did Lib or I utter. But Gus was a boy, and he refused to stand it. He said nothing to mother, but he told us that he would starve before he would eat mush and milk and go to bed at sundown. He made these remarks several times while eating his mush and milk right along, and consequently the force of his threat was weakened. But one evening he refused to eat. He said he simply would not live to be so imposed upon. Matters began to look serious. We little sisters begged him to eat; but our begging and our too evident fright strengthened his resolve to starve to death right then and there. So he began to die; and he did die according to the best light he had on that subject. He staggered around, and then fell; after which he went through the maneuvers of a chicken with its head off, flopping about fearfully, but gradually subsiding into convulsive shivers, and then perfect repose.

At first Lib and I clung to each other in inexpressible terror. Then when all was over we gave such shrieks as brought the family about us instantly. In spasmodic gasps we told what had happened. Mother marched with firm strides to where the rawhide was hanging, and was only one second in bringing the dead to life.

Whether Gus's simulated death had any effect on her or not I cannot say, but it was not long before the mush and milk suppers were abandoned, and the sun shone again in our baby lives.

But of all the youngsters who maneuvered to have their own way, Lloyd took the lead. The number of schemes he hatched, the number of escapades he engineered to certain wreck, the number of times he ran off, the number of threats he made, and the dire character of those threats, are beyond my power to recall. But for my folly in believing he would do as he threatened, I would have had more peace of mind. But it has already been shown that I was more inclined to believe my fears than my hopes, and so he kept me in hot water constantly. Once—in the height of my career as a story writer—an epoch I have not yet reached in this narrative—I wrote a sketch called "Good for Naught." It was quite a literary success. Its characters were all drawn from my home life. Among others this brother Lloyd figured in it under the name of Bill; and the incidents I described therein were the scarcely overdrawn occurrences of this boy's childhood.

It could not have been long after his visit to the "world" when he ran off and walked fifteen miles to Burnt Prairie. There he stopped at the house of a stranger, and asked to stay all night. Of course, no person could refuse the fair haired, pretty little creature, fashionably dressed, too, for that part of the world, and betraying all the marks of belonging to "quality folks," as the upper class was called; so he was welcomed politely, and on being requested "unfolded his tale." He said his name was Pete Hargroves; that his mother was a widow and lived in the northern part of the state; that he was going to

Shawneetown to become cabin boy on a steamer running from that place to New Orleans.

The next day was Sunday, and he was starting on his journey again, when his host told him what day of the week it was, adding that no one could succeed who broke the Sabbath by travelling. Lloyd was easily persuaded to delay his trip. Unfortunately for his intentions he concluded to farther placate the powers above by going with the family to Sunday school. There he met a man who traded at father's store, and who knew our children by sight.

This man I recall as one of the familiar figures of my childhood; "Old Steve Merritt." He probably was not old at all. But children look into a face of forty and recognize more age there than they can find in a face of eighty when they themselves have crossed the meridian line. Steve Merritt was one of the staunchest citizens of the country. He was a lame man, but his walk denoted great decision of character in spite of the fact.

After Mr. Merritt had some conversation with the man who brought Lloyd to the school, he then went to Lloyd and asked him who he was, and where he came from. Straight as could be Lloyd repeated the same yarn; his name was Pete Hargroves; his mother was a widow, etc. When he had finished, Mr. Merritt said, "Now, young man, I know you. You're one of Cale Wilmans' boys; and you've run off; and I'm going to tote you home." And he did. In the evening of that same day, Mr. Merritt appeared before the door on horseback, with Lloyd strapped on behind him. Poor mother who had been frantic all during his absence, succumbed and went comfortably to bed. But I was afraid to let the little villain out of my sight; and though my sight was blurred by crying until my eyes looked like two holes burnt in a red blanket, and my white eyebrows showed to more startling disadvantage than ever before, yet I kept up, and followed him wherever he went, exerting myself to entertain him, too, in spite of the fact that each pulsation of my aching head was like a blow from a hammer.

Neither of my small brothers liked to work. Put them to doing anything useful and they tired easily. Mother used to tell them that work was good for them; it loosened up the skin so they could grow. But they did not want to grow. They wanted to be dwarfs so they could go with a show and make money easily. And Lloyd would tell mother what he would buy for her when he got to be a dwarf and earned twenty-nine million dollars a week. "And when I'm goin' to be so rich you oughtn't to make me work. And I won't work neither; I'll kill myself first."

"Bless us and save us! It runs in the blood," laughed mother; and then she told him how Gus committed suicide, and was brought back to life with a switch.

"Yes," he said, "but Gus didn't know how. I'll die dead and fast. I'll make a sure enough die of it, and then you'll feel awful bad 'cause you worked me so hard."

Scarcely a day passed without this threat in one form or another, and it became a permanent joke among the town boys of his own age—who, by the way, never called him anything but "Pete Hargroves" after the run away adventure I have spoken of.

It made Lloyd mad to be called by this name, and he had fought many a fight because of it. But at last he was forced to accept it, though never willingly.

"Ain't you dead yet, Pete?" they would ask in feigned surprise at seeing him. And their leave taking, after being with him awhile, was very affecting. Some of them would weep silently, while others sobbed convulsively or blubbered out loud, "We'll never see you alive again, Pete."

This jocular way of treating the matter strengthened Lloyd's resolution, until a day came when he had been worked so outrageously human nature could hold out no longer. He had brought in three baskets of chips, had set the chairs up to the table twice, and gone to a neighbor to borrow a sleeve pattern.

"Durned if I'll stand this any longer," he said to himself as he sauntered into the parlor to be out of the way of work. "I ain't goin' to let mother run this caravan any more. I'm tired of life. It don't pay. Mother says Gus tried to die and couldn't. I know he could a died just as natural as life if mother—I ain't agoin' to call her mother. I'm agoin' to call her 'Liz' like old Pete Staten does. I know Gus could a died if mo—*Liz*—had only gumption enough to let him alone, but mothers never haves any sense any how. I've knowed this ever since I was borned. Course Gus couldn't stay dead when they was a whippin him. He's too gritty for that. Nobody'd stay dead and take a poundin'. Catch 'em at it. They'd get up and pitch in, unless they was too awful, mis'ble dead, and then nobody wouldn't pound 'em. Now, then, I'm agoin' to die dead. I ain't got nothin' to live for. Moth—*Liz*—ain't got no sense; she's a eejot. The baby's meaner than anybody, too;

squack, squack, squack, if you just crook your finger at her, and run and tell moth—*Liz*. And then there's them boys, durn 'em—'boo hoo, boo hoo—good bye, Pete, give my love to the devil when you die.' I hope there is a sure enough devil, and that he'll get every one of 'em. Durn things anyhow. I'm a agoin' to lay me down and die, and I'll do it now before mo— *Liz*—wants some more chips. Won't she be 'sprised when she comes in and finds me dead? She'll feel awful bad too, goody! goody! I'd like to be back again to hear her howl. She'll feel so bad that she'll just paw the ground and kick up. Now here goes this caravan for a long journey."

And so he stretched himself out on his back and folded his hands on his breast. (At least this was his recollection of it some years afterwards.) Then he got to wondering if there is a devil, and the thought brought him instantly to a sitting posture. This small iconoclast had always doubted the existence of the devil, and his system of reasoning on the subject was not bad. Pausing a moment as he sat there, he decided that there was nothing in it; "Cos if there was he'd a had mo—*Liz*—long ago." He laid down again and quieted himself to his last sleep; then he craned his neck up and looked along the line of his body. "Durn that hole in my knee," he whined, "it spoils the looks of the corpus; makes it appear undignant." Then he composed his epitaph:

HERE LIES THE BODY OF LLOYD WILMANS. HE WAS
   THE GOODEST LITTLE FELLER EVER LIVED—
   ONLY NOBODY DIDN'T KNOW IT. HE WOULD
    A MADE A SMARTER MAN 'N GEORGE
    WASHINGTON OR OLD SOLOMON IF HE
    HAD CONTINERED TO RESIDE IN THIS
     WORLD; BUT HIS MOTHER MADE
      HIM DO THINGS HE DIDN'T
      WANT TO DO TILL SHE
       KILLED HIM.

"That'll make her squeak," said he. "That's the pizen that'll fetch her." Then his thoughts went back to the devil. "Guess I'd better pray a little to make it safe anyhow." Rolling his eyes upward he said: "Heavenly Father, I'm a dyin'. Don't let the devil get me. I should a thought you'd a put a end to him long ago. Maybe you have. If so, bully. If not, then you can't do it too soon, 'cos you know nobody's safe with him rummagin' round loose—not even me, and I'm the goodest little boy there is—Oh! Lordy, what's that?"

He had sprung to his feet with a very red face.

The object of his excited exclamation was a dragon fly—his special abhorrence. We children called them devil's darning needles, and really thought it probable that they had some special connection with that fearful individual after whom they were named. The dragon fly had flown in through the open door, touched Lloyd's little clasped hands a moment, and fluttered against the window pane.

"Now, I've got you," said he; so he took a small leather sling out of his pocket and some shot, and began to fire at it. He had almost emptied his pocket of shot—his mouth, rather—for it was in this convenient receptacle he deposited them, when the insect careened backward in mid-air, made a side swoop almost touching his tormentor's head, and darted from the room. At this moment the sound of a voice reached him from the back alley. It was one of the boys calling him out to get another chance to tease him.

"You can 'Oh! Pete,' and 'Oh! Pete,' till you're tired," said he, stretching himself once more upon the carpet and composing his limbs in death. "There ain't no Pete as I knows of, and no Lloyd either, or won't be pretty soon. I am as good as dead already."

He had scarcely assumed this position when he

started up in horror, shouting so lustily that he brought the family about him in a hurry.

"I'm shooted! I'm shooted!" he yelled, jumping up and down in violent excitement. "I'm shooted! I'm shooted!"

Mother began to examine his body, tearing his clothes off in extreme consternation. At last it was apparent that there was no hurt on him; but still he roared, "I'm shooted! I'm shooted!"

"You little dunce," said mother, "there's nothing the matter with you."

"Oh! there is, there is," he cried; "I'm shooted! I swallered a shot!"

And this was the outcome of his suicidal intention. He was so glad when he found himself safe that he brought in a basket of chips without being asked; and he gave little Emma two of his handsomest marbles that same afternoon. To be sure he took them from her the next day, but let us not mention it. "The goodest little boy that lives" cannot be good all the time.

CHAPTER V.

BROTHER FINDLAY COMES TO TOWN.

The aptest word I can apply to myself as a child is "aliveness." I was—in my own way—tremendously alive. That this aliveness was not expressed in great bodily activity is no reason for doubting that the condition existed. It betrayed itself in my love of those things that were alive; in my appreciation of life; in my disposition to protect all living creatures. It caused me a pang to kill anything, even the things I was afraid of; as snakes, worms, etc. I seemed to enter with my own feelings into the life of the lower creatures. I had a perfect passion for flowers and all growing plants. I was the first to find out that the recently planted garden seeds had broken the mold and come through; and my heart warmed with glowing affection for every one of them. "Oh! you little things, here you are," I would think, and be as happy in welcoming them as if they had been long lost friends.

I was fond of natural history. I read it with avidity. We had a great big book on the subject in our limited collection, and I poured over it with never failing interest. I may say that I studied it; and it is the only thing I ever studied until I came to investigate the mighty subject of man. I never studied my school books. There was no life in them; nothing but dust and ashes. And yet I learned them without studying them, and slid along in my classes better than the majority of the children; but they were soon forgotten.

In the study of natural history, as given in this book, and carried out still farther by my great interest in living things, I laid the foundation of my entire future life. It was from this that I came to think of the law of growth, and man's relation to it. It was also from the study of natural history, aided by the education I had derived from "The Arabian Nights," that I began to look upon man as a being of limitless power. But all of this was crushed back and kept under for many years. The seeds of a mighty truth were buried in my mind, but the time of their appearance was not yet.

In the meantime I jogged along under the responsibility of the children, and the heavier responsibility of the religious ideas that began to be crowded upon me.

A church had been built in the town, and a preacher made regular visits. Mother soon manifested great interest in the salvation of her soul, and even went so far as to become a sort of assistant in "bringing other souls to the Savior."

It was at this point that the real wretchedness of my life commenced. I was a sinner, and no good actions of my own would count as anything in my salvation. I did not believe this, but it was finally borne in on me in spite of my mental protests, and I ceased to resist or resent it. My own reasoning powers I had good cause for doubting, and I suspended their use entirely. In doing so I became simply a reservoir for the fixed beliefs of those about me. I was still a child, and a very young child for such an awful doctrine to overtake and overwhelm.

My fairy stories were all lies, and I was a liar in repeating them. I did not know where I was or what I was, and was only conscious of an ever present distress. It was almost a sin for me to love the children as I did, and a fearful sin for me to screen them from punishment, as I had formerly done. I surely jeopardized my immortal soul every time I told a lie for them; and the necessity for these lies was greater than ever, as the bigger they became the more mischievous they grew; and mother's methods of restraint simply aggravated their tendencies, none of which were bad, though they all ran in the direction of breaking rules established for their restraint.

I had come under the dominion of a great fear. I had lost the foot-hold of self, and was adrift. There was a constant internal unrest. It was as if some latent power imprisoned in my breast was tearing me to pieces in order to escape.

Even now I wonder what it was. Is reincarnation true? I am told that many persons have proof that seems positive to them, that they existed in the human form before their present incarnation. I cannot say this of myself; and yet I have mental idiosyncrasies that seem to refer to events that might have occurred ages and ages ago. But in trying to recall these far away happenings I get the idea that I was not then in the human form; or, if in the human form, that my brain was of the crudest character; for with all such retrospection there comes a numbness of the reasoning faculties, and an all pervading fear of calamity, as if my life at that time had been in the midst of untold terrors.

Upon being put to bed I rarely failed to see strange creatures, part human and part animal, and I was afraid of them. That these forms were real I do not doubt. I have since learned that everything is substance, and that there is no nothing; therefore, all the forms that are attributed to an overwrought imagination are substantial forms. Possibly they are thought forms, and the imagination may produce them; but for the time they exist they are tangible entities. It may be they are so frail that a breath can dissolve them, and they may not under any circumstance possess enough power to lift a hair, but they are surely real so long as they exist. I am inclined to think that I created the forms of which I was so afraid; though there are persons to whom I have related these experiences who believe them to be the spirits of animals not yet arrived at incarnation in the human shape.

But, whatever their cause, they followed me, very much against my will, far along into my maturer years. In spite of the uneasiness they always gave me, I am glad to have had my experience with them. I believe they have taught me one of the greatest lessons of my life; namely, that thought has power to create without the use of the hands, and also without employing any *visible* means in doing it.

I say "visible" means, because means will be used. Things cannot be created without something to create with; but this something is invisible on the dull plane of sense in which our faculties now preside. It will belong to the unseen and unexplored forces that surely do exist, and are even now inviting our investigation.

And this suggests the possibility that the East India fakir is simply a person, who, by long training in one direction, and by an inherited propensity for this peculiar training, does actually possess the power in some degree to create by his thought.

It is well known that these fakirs are the descendants of long lines of fakirs; men who have given their attention to nothing else, and have thus come into possession of more power in this particular thing than ordinary men.

At the same time I do not believe that they themselves understand the power they use. From close observation of the conditions essential to a manifestation of the power, they have learned what to do in order to bring about certain results; but I feel confident that the law underlying the manifestations is a dead letter to them.

To illustrate: A fakir or magician comes out into the open space where five thousand persons are assembled to witness his performance. He takes a ball of twine and throws it up into the air; he holds one end of the twine, and the ball unwinds as it goes up; it goes up so high that it is out of sight. He then calls his assistant and tells him to go up and bring the ball down; the assistant begins to climb the twine, and keeps ascending until he too is out of sight. Presently the magician calls to him to come down; but he does not come. Then he begins to climb the twine himself, evidently intending to bring the boy down dead or alive. The spectators meanwhile are almost breathless in astonishment. *They are intensely concentrated on the performance.*

A few minutes after the magician has disappeared in the upper air, one leg of the boy is thrown down; then the other leg, and an arm, etc., until the entire body has been dissected and dropped to the ground, where it is covered by a coarse cloth. Then the magician descends winding the ball of twine as he comes. Last of all the boy crawls out from under his covering entirely uninjured.

Five thousand men have been looking on, and they all saw the thing the same way. Did the magician have power to hypnotize all this body of men, and make them believe they saw things that had no existence?

It seems more reasonable to believe that he had

power to literally clothe his thoughts out of the elements present on the ground, and cause them to take shape for the time. Furthermore, it may be that these elements were human elements furnished him by the men present. These men had virtually let go of themselves through the power of expectation, and had become almost unconscious of their existence. In this negative attitude the life element within them was, in a measure, under obedience to the magician's thought, and clothed his thought, thus rendering it a tangible thing, to be seen by all persons during the few moments it lasted.

I read not long ago that an attempt had been made to photograph these appearances while they were in existence, and that the effort had failed. This may have been true or it may not. But even if the effort were made, it must be remembered that the kodak is not a reliable instrument; and that many of the plates on which a picture is expected to appear remain blank from a failure to get a perfect focus. The fact is, this matter has never been submitted to any kind of scientific test at all, and no one knows the philosophy of it. But there is a philosophy connected with it, and it comes within the range of natural law. We shall understand it sometime.

Yesterday I was reading an article on this subject, and some of the statements were really so miraculous as to be almost beyond the possibility of belief. "What nonsense!" I thought. And then I thought again. "Why," said I to myself, "it is this thing of doubting statements without investigating them that has so limited our intelligence and our knowledge at this time. I am going to quit doubting. Better be fooled a thousand times by over believing than to be a fool forever by not believing at all."

At this juncture in came Mrs. Louisa Southworth, to whom I read what I have written on the East India performances, as recorded above.

"Is it not possible," asked she, "that the magician so concentrates the minds of his vast audience on what he is doing, *or the thought he is projecting*, rather, that they see his thought with the mind's eye while it is entirely invisible to the eye of the more negative body? This," she continued, "would account for the fact that they could not photograph it."

Mrs. Southworth's assumption puts the entire performance on a psychological basis. If correct it would be an added proof that thoughts are things, and that man can so divorce his finer, less material thought from the coarser and more inert, as to see thought forms. If this is true the performance could be photographed, but not by the common camera; it would require a more delicate invention, which reminds me that a machine for photographing thought has recently been invented and stood the test of experiment well. But no such machine as this has been used for the purpose above recorded.

I have been diverging from my story. I must confine myself still longer to the life I passed in the little old town where I was born, and where nearly all the friends of those days lie buried.

I visited this place in 1883, after thirty years absence. There was scarcely a soul left of all those I had once known. The town had grown into a beautiful place, full of handsome residences; and the locomotive had superseded the old four-horse stage, whose coming and going had once been the leading event of the week.

One day as I was walking along a beautifully shaded street (during the visit of which I have been speaking) there came a voice behind me calling my name, and the sound of hurried footsteps with it. I turned to meet the dark, handsome face of a stalwart stranger. He caught me by both hands. "Don't you know me, Helen, don't you know me?" he asked. I did not know him. "Don't you remember little Charley Brown?" I tried hard to recall him. "Many's the night," he went on, "that I have slipped out of the window after mother put me to bed, and run to the hall where the dance was going on, on purpose to see you dance. I was dead in love with you in those days, and your utter indifference kept my little fool heart in the most abjectly tattered condition imaginable."

I was a grown young lady at that time, and Charley a cub of eight years. That he had recognized me at all after so long a period was a matter of surprise and congratulation.

The log house in which I was born was still standing, and probably it is there yet. But the town was the saddest place I ever saw. Nearly all the old friends were dead, and those who remained seemed even more dead than those who were buried. As a feeble light in a dark place simply renders the darkness more visible, so the small amount of life left in these old friends of mine seemed to register the lifelessness of their condition. Wherever I met one of them the question came up, "Have you seen Nancy Marks yet?" And then there was a laugh of derision. Nancy had been a butt for ridicule in the old school days. I went to see her, and soon knew why they laughed at her. She was the only soul among them who had gained a new idea in all these years. She was so far ahead of the others that they almost believed her to be insane. She had been a very homely girl. She was now, in my eyes, the handsomest woman in town. Her face was radiant with the light of a growing soul; and, oh, what a contrast with the other faces I met!

My pretty little sister Lib, who helped me fight aunt Sally Linthecum in defense of Gus, was living there. She had married a merchant of the town and was "powerful fore-handed," living in a house with a mansard-roof. Both herself and husband were members of an orthodox church, and were firmly convinced that I was on the straight road to the devil. Indeed, Lib had been convinced of this many years before my visit. At one time I had sent her some papers that were an advancement on the old lines of thought, and they had frightened her. I expect she took my case to Jesus and agonized over it for a week before she made up her mind what course to pursue. Then she wrote me. She asked what I supposed mother would have thought of my permitting a paper, such as I had sent her, to come into my house. It was a long letter full of reproaches, and also of doubts of my character. It wound up by reference to my children. She said she was sorry for them, and thought I had better send them to her to bring up.

I thought of this when I looked at her children. They possessed a measure of superficial good looks, but they were a different type from mine. How could I help contrasting their faces with the unusual faces of the grown up children I had left in California, whose whole lives had been an acquisition of new and positive truth, and whose physical organizations showed the power of such truth to mold the external.

I went to this place to spend the summer. I remained there six days.

There is no doubt that a low state of intelligence produces negative people who are comparatively powerless to resist disease. At the time I was a child and lived in this town, the status of intelligence was much lower than it was when I returned on the visit I have described. But the new people were strangers to me. The old ones had taken the consequence of their ignorance, and were either dead or dying. There were progressive people in the town, as there are in all towns of its size at this day; and I do not mean to leave the impression that it was not fully up to other places of its class, but simply to show that the few old friends I had left were not among the progressive ones, but had stood in the same tracks all the years of my absence.

When I first remember old Fairfield there was no preacher there, and no religious privileges beyond the range of aunt Sally's slipper; but the dismal day of the preacher's advent dawned in the course of time. His name was Findlay. He was a gentle, soft-spoken man, tall and slender and pale, who used "scriptor" language in his conversation wherever he could. He came once in three weeks to our town, and preached on Saturday night and Sunday morning. I remember his asking me one evening after preaching—he was stopping with us—if the Lord had blessed the discourse to my uplifting. I was only a little thing, and I looked him in the face earnestly, hoping some light would shine from his eyes that might make the meaning of his words clear. Then he asked me if I liked the "serming." Heaven only knows what inspired me to tell him the truth. It surely was not the force of habit.

"No, sir," I said, "I didn't like it at all."

"Why, Helen," said mother, "what was the matter with the sermon?"

I said it was too long.

He smiled at mother in a very indulgent way, and said to me, but with his look really directed to her, "Now, my dear little girl, when you hear me delivering the word of God again, and feel that I am becoming prosy and uninterestin', and that it is time to stop, you just hold up your hand."

This piece of facetiousness cost me a whipping the very next day. I was sitting close by mother in the court house, where the brother was holding forth at his morning performance, and I was tired. I was always tired of the Lord's day and all its practices. On this occasion the preacher had hardly reached "secondly" out of about nineteen of his headings, when I began to wiggle my hand in the most energetic manner, literally shaking the bench on which we were sitting. Brother Findlay saw me and was embarrassed, and could hardly proceed. Then mother saw me and gave me a look that brought me to order. After we got home she took down the switch and paid me for my folly in supposing that preachers were more truthful than other people. In time I came to look back on this whipping as the most salutary and educational of any I had ever received.

CHAPTER VI.

AT A CATHOLIC SCHOOL.

On one occasion when brother Findlay came it was late, almost time for his Saturday night's audience to assemble. Mother had been sent for by a sick neighbor, but expected to return soon. It was fearfully cold and he had ridden forty miles, having lost his way in a snow storm. He was as prolific of scriptural sentences as usual. As he stood thawing out before the fire he turned to me in a grave way and said:

"My little sister, I have fasted since mornin' and would fain beg a little bread and water."

What he meant was fried chicken, hot biscuit, preserves and coffee; but how was I to know? My father took the baby out of my arms with unusual alacrity, and a look of preternatural solemnity. It was a look that always made me uneasy, even though I had not then learned that it resulted from an effort to keep from laughing.

I went into the cheerless dining room and set the table. I put a pitcher of water, a tumbler and a loaf of bread on it. I hurried back and brought Mr. Findlay out, and there I left him and went into the warm sitting room again. Father questioned me apparently in deep dejection, frequently turning his face away. Then mother came, and finding Mr. Findlay's hat and overcoat, began to question father.

"He is all right, Lib," father assured her; "sit down and get warm; and take the baby; he needs you; he is sleepy."

"But, Caleb, who got brother Findlay's supper?"

"Helen got it, and"—

"Helen!" sneered mother. "The idea of her getting supper! Did you see what she had on the table?"

"I didn't look at the table, but he told her what to get. Now don't go, Lib; you're cold. I'll go myself. You take the baby; he has the colic. Don't you see how pale he looks?"

Mother would not be detained. She rushed into the dining room where she found the disgusted preacher shivering over his dreadful supper. She brought him back to the fire, and made him comfortable while she cooked him a royal meal.

When it was all over I was threatened with the whip. But father put his hand on it where it hung against the wall. "Not to-night, Lib," he said. His handsome face, always frank and tender, looked quite grave, though not stern.

I know so little of my father. He was a humorous man. He saw the comical side of everything. He managed to get a good deal of fun out of the children; but we were a little bit afraid of his laugh. He must have known this, and being one of Nature's truest gentlemen, he often tried to conceal it from us. This accounts for the unnatural solemnity of expression he occasionally wore. He had his opinion of preachers and religion, and maintained it to the last. A few times only I heard him express himself about them. He did it in the most laughable manner imaginable. Even mother could not keep her face straight, though she would make every effort to silence him. I never heard him speak seriously on the subject but once. He was talking to mother. He said, "We used to have such good times, Lib, before you joined the church and became absorbed in saving souls. It is all changed now. You are not the same woman, and the children are not the same. There is an awful shadow over the household."

The stage from Carmi came in once a week, and it was a grand event. It brought a few letters and papers, and occasionally some passengers. We children used to swarm out on the road to meet it, and often the driver would take us up and give us a ride.

Later, when I was considered too large a girl for such sport, I would be permitted to go to the hotel, and there, sitting on an upper porch with Nannie Wood, the hotel keeper's daughter, we watched the passengers alight and took note of their dress and appearance. This was among our most exciting pleasures.

One afternoon while watching, a strange couple alighted; or, rather, a strange trio, for there were three of them; and perhaps no persons in all the world have had so distinct an influence in my development as they had.

But I must go back to circumstances which happened before this, and then work up to the advent of these new acquaintances.

I cannot recall my exact age when mother resolved to send me to a Catholic school in a distant state. I did not want to go, but that was of no consequence; I had to go; but I soon made up my mind that I would get away as quickly as I could. I knew my parents did not know the secret workings of the place, or they would not have kept me there. It was impossible to communicate with them as to anything derogatory to the institution. Our letters were all read before being sent out, and I never received one while there that had not been broken open.

Ordinarily we were treated well enough. There was nothing to complain of in regard to our accommodation. The fare, though plain, was wholesome and abundant, and our beds were comfortable, though about one hundred of us slept in a single, large, well ventilated room. I loved the most of the nuns, who were our teachers, and had nothing to complain of with regard to their treatment. There was one of them, however, who was very cruel, and who punished us unmercifully. I only had occasion to come under her wrath once, and I do not doubt but the event is as memorable to her as to me. She was a small woman and of Irish nationality. She sat in the common school room to preserve order. Occasionally a girl was sent into the dormitory, and told to wait there until she came.

One day she sent me up there. On my way I picked up a kitten. How it came to be there I have no idea, since every such thing was carefully excluded from the building. But there it was on the stair steps, and I was so glad to see it that I could not love it enough. I carried it up with me, and nursed it to sleep, and laid it on a bed close by. I was not anticipating a whipping in the least, and was quite unprepared to see sister Martha bounce into the room with one of the cruelest rawhide whips I had ever seen.

Her quick eye fell on the kitten. "Who brought this thing up here?" she asked.

"I did, sister Martha. Don't wake it up," I pleaded.

She caught it by the tail, and holding it at arms' length began to beat it with such dexterous rapidity as to stupefy my wits for the moment; then she threw it from the open window, by which I was sitting. I leaned out to see the tortured creature drag itself under the house as if its back was broken. A whole tide of rage was surging up within me, which I would have suppressed but for what followed.

It was summer time and we children wore low-necked and short-sleeved dresses. Before I had drawn back from the window, she struck me on the bare neck and shoulder savagely and with lightning-like rapidity. In righting my position I struck my head on the window sash in a way that dazed me. I got my fleeing senses back with a tremendous effort; an effort that nearly cost sister Martha her life.

What happened I never distinctly knew. I jumped on her and bore her down with my weight. I was an enormously large child and my strength was phenomenal. I tore her cap off and pounded her unmercifully as I knelt on her back and churned her with my knees. Then I came to my senses, and was frightened. It was my screams, not hers, that brought the nuns about us. The priest came and took me away through many rooms and passages blindfolded; and then locked me into a dungeon where I remained for several days.

Once a day a slide was opened and a pitcher of water and loaf of bread were placed on a table close by.

There was a very hard bed in there and a pillow. I cannot at all remember what my thoughts were; but being a child of fertile imagination and inexhaustible hope, I bore the situation with wonderful fortitude. I recall this fact perfectly. I did not cry nor waste any effort in screaming; I sat on the side of the bed a long time, and then lay down and fell asleep. When I awoke I was unconscious of whether it was night or day. The strain I put upon my eyes to see gave me the impression that I was blind. Then I relaxed my effort and the strain passed away, leaving me in a peculiar frame of mind.

I had always played with dolls. I have never yet seen a child so fond of them as I was. It had been a hard thing for me to be deprived of them in coming to this school, and often of a night I would take one of my garments and roll it into one and hold it all night long. I was horribly lonesome in a dumb way, but bore everything patiently.

Being in the dungeon and thrown on my own devices, I took off a skirt and made a doll of it; and oh, what a comfort it was to me! My love nature awakened, and with it my imagination. I began to see things in the dark. At first what I saw was only a series of colored balls descending from above and disappearing as they neared the floor. The colors on them changed almost constantly. After a time the balls came in flocks, and then in showers. In the course of a day or two I was surrounded by the most indescribably beautiful sights that ever were witnessed. Now, it was a fountain of the most graceful form, throwing its glittering and many colored jewels up, up, a hundred feet in the air, from whence it tumbled in cataracts of such luminous and glorious colors that no pen can describe them. There were colors that never yet have been seen, and forms that no person in real life has conceived of.

Sometimes for hours there would be a series of geometrical figures made out of diamonds and rubies and other precious stones. Then again these brilliant jewels would be woven into flowers and trees and shrubbey. Again, long isles would open in this vast maze of glittering shrubbery, and other scenes in the distance would appear. I saw nothing that was alive, as birds or human beings. It was all still life, but so changeful and so wonderful that I did not once tire of looking at it. I ate my bread and drank my water, but never spoke to the person who brought it. After a certain length of time had expired, the priest who superintended the establishment came to the opening and asked me if I was ready to ask sister Martha's pardon for my offense. I refused to answer. He waited awhile and then left. It was not long before he repeated the visit. Again I refused to answer. After this performance had been enacted three or four times, the door opened and he came in with a lantern and dragged me out quite blinded with the light. I was taken to a room on the upper floor where a number of the nuns were assembled, and there I was forced to promise under fearful threats never to tell that I had been in the dungeon. And so this episode ended.

Soon after this, one of the elder girls disappeared from the class room. It was said that she was sick. She was a sulky, disagreeable girl, and very little inquiry was made concerning her. But a few days after her disappearance, I myself was in the infirmary quite ill with the mumps, and through a half open door I saw her led into the room adjoining mine. She was in a deplorable condition, white as a corpse, and so weak it took two of the nuns to support her.

The door was closed between us, but by some oversight it was left unlocked; so I watched my opportunity and went in. She too had been in the dungeon and the awful punishment had almost killed her. She lingered for weeks on the verge of death, but finally recovered.

During this time there was an epidemic of sickness in the school, and some of the household servants were promoted to the position of nurses. By promises, the girl I am writing of, got one of them to furnish her with pencil and paper, on which she wrote a few urgent words to her father. This was conveyed secretly to the post-office, and did its work. Her father came and took her home. Later still he sent four officers there to investigate the building. But they failed to find the dungeon; and everything was peaceful once more. I longed to tell those men all about it, but not one moment was I free from the surveillance of the nuns.

It might be supposed that I had my privileges

curtailed after whipping sister Martha. On the contrary, it seemed to be the sister whose privileges were curtailed. She was more gentle in the school room, and I fancied she was treated less courteously by the other sisters. As for me, I was "cock of the walk" from that time on. I think it likely that the other sisters hated her, and were glad she had gotten whipped.

I cannot tell why it was, but for some reason or other I was greatly petted and favored in the school by both nuns and the father confessor who frequently came among us. Some of the girls got down on their knees and kissed the hem of his long black robe, as he passed through the school room. All of them arose to their feet except me. All I ever did was to hide the novel I was reading and gaze on him quietly. I had no intention of being disrespectful, but my father had been in the habit of rising from his chair when his little daughters entered the room, and providing us with seats before sitting down again himself. So it was simply a sort of second nature that kept me seated. My conduct was not reproved; and the priest would approach me smiling and shake hands with me. I never saw him offer to shake hands with any other girl.

I read my first novel here. It was "Alonzo and

Melissa." It was a tame thing to me after the "Arabian Nights," and the many supplements to the "Arabian Nights," that I myself had added. But all the girls were reading it and deeply excited over it. The only enjoyment I got out of it was in the fact that it was stolen fun. I suppose I thought I was trampling sister Martha's immortal soul in the dirt by sitting in her very presence and reading that trash instead of studying my lesson.

"You dreadful old thing," I used to think as I looked at her; "you know you are afraid to take this book from me." At the same time I concealed it from her sight quite carefully.

We were compelled to attend mass whether we wanted to or not; and the devotional services of each day in the week were excessive. We were made to kneel bolt upright for an hour at a time every morning, giving the responses to prayers that one of the sisters read. How tired we became! frequently one of the weaker girls fainted dead away and was carried out limp as a rag. I was too strong for any such exhibition; and in the course of time my knees became so callous that I could kneel as easily as I could stand.

I neglected to tell in its proper place of how—on the day Sister Martha sent me up into the dormitory to wait for her coming—that I got restless after the cat went to sleep and began to prospect for something to do. I soon found a decanter of holy water with which I was quite familiar, having heard its merits extolled by the Catholic girls and the nuns also. It had played an important part in saving the sick from dying, and in keeping souls out of Purgatory, etc. I think I had considerable respect for the stuff, though I was not quite certain of it until some two weeks later. However, with one of the sudden lapses into imbecility to which I think I was subject at that age, I poured the water out of the decanter upon the head of a girl in the yard below, and then filled it up again out of one of the pitchers. I felt no more compunction in committing this piece of *diablerie* than if I had been a Newfoundland puppy.

But when—a few nights after I was released from the dungeon—a perfectly terrific thunder storm arose, and the priest was sent for to pray and sprinkle the beds with holy water, and I saw him using my substitute for the real stuff, I was frightened and awaited results with great anxiety. As the storm soon stopped I suppose the Virgin Mary, to whom the adjurations were addressed, did not know the difference; but it was a trick I never ventured to repeat. It was not long after this, in the communion services the priest discovered that the silver dish which had always held the holy bread or wafers to be administered on that solemn occasion was empty. I do not remember what was substituted for them, nor how the matter ended. I do know, however, that neither Emma Ready nor I thought they tasted good, and we would not have eaten them only we had heard repeatedly that they turned to blood on the tongue of an unsanctified person. We evidently wanted to investigate this claim.

Vacation came and there was a general exodus. It had been decided by my parents that I was not to return home for another year. This was dreadful for me to bear, and I did not intend to bear it. Mr. Ready, who lived in Carmi, just twenty-five miles from Fairfield, came for Emma in a carriage. I was only permitted to see him in the presence of one of the nuns; but I communicated with him by means of his daughter.

There were so many carriages coming and going through the great iron gates that day, I contrived to slip out and hide by the roadside a half mile away. At this spot Mr. Ready picked me up, and it was good-bye to that school forever. I left my trunk and all I had except the clothes I wore, and never recovered them, though there was an effort made to do so.

I met my mother in Carmi. She was on a visit to my grandfather and grandmother. She had with her the baby I had never seen, little Julia; this child and her twin sister, who was then dead, had been born a day or two after I left home. How I had longed to see this new baby, and how I had cried when I knew there had been two of them, and only one alive.

A few years later I was at Emma Ready's wedding. She was a girl of great expectations and much wealth for that day and part of the country. She married a brilliant lawyer, and no one doubted the promise of her young life. It was only ten months afterwards that she lay in her coffin with her dead baby on her breast.

Is every one of these chapters to end in a grave?

CHAPTER VII.

THE DALTON EPISODE.

It was some time after I got home from the Catholic school before the old interests took hold of me again. The baby was not my baby, and I did not like it much. It had only weighed two and one-half pounds when it was born, and at the time I first saw it, was the smallest, most inferior little thing I ever looked at. Its head was too big and its hands and feet not big enough. But it was the spunkiest and the most precocious youngster of the lot. Grandfather Ridgway—the father of my mother and of little aunt Mary—doted on this poor little, saucy little, ugly little fragment of humanity. He would always have it in his arms when he was in the house. It could talk before it was eleven months old, and walked sometime before that.

Grandfather was a Whig in politics, and seemed to take endless interest in the newspapers. I can see him with his glasses on his nose as he sat by the window with a paper in one hand and this mite of a baby tucked away in his other arm, she reaching out as far as possible and wriggling from every position he assigned her for the purpose of kicking the paper to make it rattle.

"Now, Jule," he would say, "you must not do that; grandpa 'll have to spank. See my big hand?" And then he would show her a large, fair hand, corresponding with the large, fair body that owned it.

"Me'll pank oo," the little vixen would retort; "tee my bid hand?" showing a hand about like a sparrow's claw. Then grandfather would laugh a laugh that could be heard the other side of town, and roar out for mother to come and witness the performance, which the graceless baby would enact as often as called upon.

More than once I have seen him go over to the saloon, where men were usually congregated, and set her on the counter, when he would produce the paper, and the two would again rehearse the scene whose only claim to comicality lay in the contrast between the baby's threats and her weapons for executing them. By this time her threats had been so greatly exaggerated under the tutelage of those two past master generals in deviltry—Lloyd and Ivens—as to be actually bloodthirsty and terrifying.

"Me'll till oo; me'll frow oo on ee floor and pull oor legs out and pound oo to def wid em; tee my bid hands? Oo'd better be dood." And all the time she was saying these things she would be striking him in the breast with blows equal in force to those of a mouse's tail; and her little feet—not much bigger than a hard shell June bug—would be kicking him with indescribable vigor.

"Aint she got the sand?" he would ask between his explosions of laughter. And then he would expostulate with her, begging her to spare his life, which only made her more frantic in her display of muscular force.

I recall a particular day when grandfather had just come to our house after an absence of several months. The news that grandpa Ridgway had come flew like lightning through the town; and if he had been a lump of sugar and the children ants, the effect would not have been different. They came pouring into our front porch from every direction; dozens of them; not only the "quality" children, but poor little distressed mites, the victims of the malarious climate and of poverty, their faces showing every particle of the small amount of sunshine the weakened action of their hearts could generate. And it was, "Howdy do, piggy-wees; ha, ha, ha, but grandpa's glad to see you; and here's my little Maggie, and here's Mahaly, and here's Tom. Well, bless my life! Ha, ha, ha, this is a regular ovation; and here are more small people coming still;" and he broke away from the crowd surrounding him and strode out with his mighty steps and his superb strength to pick up a crippled child who was laboring across the street to give him greeting.

"Why its grandpa's little sweetheart, aint it? Its my dear little Sallie; and she hasn't forgotten me either, has she? Well bless her soul and body; and she's growing big, too, and heavy; my stars, how heavy she is!" And all the time the little lame creature was clinging to him with tender eyes full of unspeakable love.

This little one paid the penalty of her frailness soon after. But Jule, the hero of so many mimic frays, is not only alive and well at this time, but crows over the other four sisters because she is the tallest one of them all. A small body did not seem to count against the irrepressible spirit that infused it.

Reference has been made to a certain afternoon when Nanny Wood and I sat on an upper balcony at her father's hotel and watched the stage come in.

As the dust-covered vehicle stopped, the door swung open and a young man with a large forehead got out. Then a baby was poked out to him which he took hold of awkwardly; last a woman or child—not looking more than sixteen—climbed out backwards and turning round took a languid survey of the house. She had on a white swiss mull dress with pink ribbon garniture. Her eyes were large and pensive and dark, and her hair was black as midnight and hung in profuse curls far below her waist line. She was very dusty and "mussy" in her appearance, but she was wonderfully pretty and looked more like a fancy picture than a real woman.

Mrs. Wood brought the trio up stairs and gave them a room opening on the veranda where Nan and I were sitting. The baby kept up an unbroken cry that hurt the little mother heart of me; and presently from the sound of the voices inside I knew that there was more than one of them crying.

I was never a bold child, but I thought I knew that I could relieve the baby, and so I summoned all my courage and knocked at the door. "Please let me take the baby," I said; "I can quiet him; I am used to babies."

"Are you? Oh, dear! I am not; I don't know

what to do with him," said his little mother, still crying like a baby herself, which she really was.

I took the child down stairs into the kitchen and got some warm water, into which I plunged him up to his neck. He was dirty and neglected and chafed until the raw flesh was in an awful condition. I worked with him an hour, and finally by the aid of cooling restoratives and by powdering him with starch I made him comfortable and happy. Mrs. Wood found some little slips that had belonged to one of her babies years back, and brought them to me. Nan tore up some old sheets into napkins for him, for actually he seemed to have almost no changes of clothes at all.

When I carried him back he was cooing cheerfully, and presently fell asleep and slept for hours.

The next day the baby was crying again and could not be soothed. Then this little mother found out where I lived, and brought the child to me. She looked fresher than on her arrival, but had on another ball room costume, her dress being a pink tarlatan trimmed with white ribbon. She was evidently afraid of mother, and only at home with me. For my part I was a little afraid of her; for I saw instantly that she was a college bred girl, and I felt my ignorance in her presence. But I knew more about babies than she did; and I perceived that she attached so great an importance to this fact that she was ready to doff all her laurels before my superiority in the only knowledge she now valued.

Friendships ripen rapidly between young people. My new friend was several years older than I, but did not seem to know it. "You see you know so much," she said, "you really might be forty years old. I have never seen such true wisdom in one so young. I do hope you will like me and be my friend, for I am already so in love with you. I have never met such a grand girl."

Now, this was praise indeed, and I drank it in joyously. That this beautiful woman, who could paint pictures and play the piano and write poems, should say such things about me, and believe them too, for she did believe them—being but a helpless little puss after all—was just the cordial I needed to strengthen every faculty of my mind, and to awaken new faculties undreamed of before.

In the story of "Good for Naught," one of my literary successes, I have described this Dr. Dalton, and I will reproduce the description here:

"He was educated for a physician. He thought

himself a mechanical genius, and really was one, if he could have stuck to anything long enough to make a success of it. In reality he was fit for nothing at all, unless it might be an angel. It is not positively asserted that he was fit for that. If, however, the absence of evil, the negative virtue of harmlessness, together with a happy disposition are the requisite attributes, the idea occurs that he might have been intended 'to loaf around the throne,' as John Hay expresses it, and that he would have answered in that capacity as well as a better man. At all events, he had no capacity for getting along in this wooden world. He was a busy fellow, always working at something of no possible utility, and neglecting his practice to do it.

"He made models of impossible machines; he had a model quartz mill with ever so many stamps in it. It came in time to be used as the family coffee mill—the whole family collecting about it every morning to watch the little stamps as they pounded the grains of coffee into powder. He had a model reaping machine which could be made to mow its way through a cabbage head, in consequence of which cold-slaw became a favorite dish among them. He had a model steamship, and other models, constructed out of cigar boxes principally, and nearly all of them unfinished, or finished so lingeringly that the latter end of them appeared to have forgotten the beginning.

"The doctor made the same impression on an observant person that his models did. He was unfinished; he was all there, but there was not a solitary rivet to fasten his faculties in position; and in the general mixing up of him since his birth, nature seemed to have forgotten the original intention of his design. He had the brightest, most interested and innocent eyes ever seen; his forehead was large and bare; and as he had but the segment of a nose like a baby's, and a rudimentary mouth like a tadpole's, he created the belief that he had been born prematurely and had never caught up."

At an early age, while yet a college student in Louisville, Kentucky, he had run away with, and married a pretty school girl who had never perpetrated the first useful act in her mortal life. When the boy's father heard of it and went after the little fools, he found them up four flights in a seven-by-nine room under the roof, vowing eternal constancy throughout all the heavenly future, without enough money between them to buy a scuttle of coal. The sight of his helpless boy and the beautiful child wife disarmed his anger, and being a jolly old soul his vengeance ended in laughter.

"Here's richness," quoth he; "married in Lilliput and keeping house under a cabbage leaf."

He did what he could for them time and again, and finally sent them way out on the borders of civilization to get rid of them.

"I guess you'll not starve, Jack," he said; "there's a special providence for fools and children, and you can claim protection under either clause of the provision."

And so they landed out of the stage in old Fairfield that summer afternoon, where the doctor began to tinker the neighbor's bodies when he could spare time from his toys, which was a great annoyance to him; so great that he was frequently known to hide under the bed when a knock that sounded at all ominous came upon the door, while his little wife met the visitor and serenely lied about her husband's absence.

She had been but sixteen years old, while her venerable husband was approaching the dotage of twenty-one, when the baby put in an appearance. And a venturesome infant he must have been to come into life under the guardianship of those other infants—his parents. And yet, with what must be regarded as an inherited recklessness of consequences, he had hurried along like other bald-headed tyrants from "No-man's Land," even laughing at the forebodings of the wise, and conducting himself with an irrepressible jollity highly reprehensible under the circumstances.

Mrs. Dalton had a great dread of the mature matrons of the place, but she clung to me with an intensity of girlish affection characteristic of that youthful age. I was surprised and flattered by her preference, and secretly thought her the loveliest and brightest of human beings—aunt Mary being at a young ladies finishing school and quite out of my life at this time.

It is no wonder that Mrs. Dalton captivated the awakening fancy of an imaginative child like me. She was a new revelation. She could play the piano, though there was not one within twenty miles of the place; yet she could play it, and that meant so much. She had a guitar on which she played, and her voice was exquisite. She could compose poetry; real poetry. I would not be sure of this only by knowing that George D. Prentice of the *Louisville Journal* bought it and paid for it. He was a poet himself and a judge of a poem's merits.

She painted in oil and in water colors, and could

make excellent likenesses of people. She often painted my picture and praised the coloring of my hair and complexion, so that I almost forgot I was not the family beauty. She really had very great genius for drawing. Her little hands flew over the paper, and the beautiful forms of nature sprang like magic beneath them. She was a strangely gifted creature, this young wife, without one practical idea in the world. She knew nothing about cooking, housekeeping or the care of her child. I, having been brought up in an orderly family, knew all these things theoretically, though so far I had not made much application of my knowledge. But now here was some one who seemed in a measure dependent upon my superior ability; who regarded my few practical accomplishments as evidences of amazing wisdom. This flattered me, and caused me to attempt the dizziest heights of housewifery. Sometimes when pressed by necessity I even tried bread baking. However, as these attempts were rather too much for my natural laziness, I usually smuggled it from mother's pantry and carried it to them.

I remember the first meal in the house after they went to housekeeping. I got it. It was about my second attempt in this direction, my first being brother Findlay's supper. We had ham and eggs. I knew how to fry ham, and felt that there was no insurmountable obstruction between me and the cooking of eggs. Mrs. Dalton helped me, doing everything I told her to do most obediently. We had a new tin coffee pot and made some tea in it. Mother had sent down some preserved fruit and a pie and pickles. But when we sat down to the table there was no bread. Actually the intensity of my chagrin at this discovery is beyond description. It seemed as if my character was ruined. Ordinarily I did not care much what people thought of me; but it was different with these people. They had descended into my life from another sphere. They brought the glory of a big city with them; and I had never seen a city, but believed that the wonders revealed by Aladdin's lamp were tame in comparison.

And these people had looked on me as a wonder in my way. I dare say I had enhanced their good opinion of my practical ability as a housekeeper by the use of the "long bow" whenever occasion offered. And now I was caught. The affair seemed tragical. All I could say was, "I will bring some bread," as I snatched my sunbonnet and started up the long dusty street. It was too great a distance to go home.

Dinner would be cold before I could return. Polly Gibson lived in the nearest cottage, and she had always been good to me; I would go there and ask for some.

I entered her house by the back way. It appeared to be empty. The kitchen was beautifully clean; the smell of new bread loaded the air. The stove door stood open and the golden brown loaves were showing fine crinkles on the sides. I did not wait one second. I turned them into my apron and ran down the back walk and out of the gate and away. I had not been five minutes gone when we drew up to the table again. Mrs. Dalton said the supper was perfectly elegant, and the doctor praised it also. But I knew more about that supper than I ever told.

The disappearance of Polly's bread was a mighty event for that small town, and continued to be a subject of conversation off and on for years. As there were no tramps in those days and no one to suspect, the affair became clothed in an atmosphere of superstition, and eventually gave Polly a spiritual halo, which, though unseen, had a tendency to put her in the category of saints, thus increasing the public respect for her. If Mrs. Dalton and the doctor had their suspicions they never mentioned them; and the probability is that if they had known the truth it would only have been regarded as another triumph of my practical ability. But I can honestly say that this is all the stealing I ever did in my life. Of course what I stole from our own pantry and carried to this family of children does not count.

It is inconceivable to what an extent mother would have opened her eyes could she have seen how industriously I worked for the Daltons. At home I could not stir up a spoonful of thickening without "making such a muss" that she would rather do it herself than clean up after me. Another duty I shouldered was making the Dalton's clothes. Had any one related this as a fact to my mother it would have been received with laughing derision; still it was true. I could not be trusted to hem a dish towel at home, but here I boldly cut into the raw material and brought forth dresses and all manner of garments for the baby. It goes without saying that our own baby was always with me in my visits to the Daltons, otherwise I could not have spent so much time there.

Little Charley's dresses—the way I made them— were models of simplicity. They were mere slips puckered into shape with a drawing string in the top, and sleeveless. It was a style of dress to be appreciated in hot weather, and the baby frequently showed his appreciation of it by snaking it off over his head at the risk of choking himself, and going naked. It seems hard to believe, but by the time he could talk and walk this young iconoclast, this breaker of customs, if not of images, was so thoroughly imbued with the family traits as to be perfectly satisfied in the garb of Cupid, and but for the compulsion which I put upon him would never have worn a dress at all. "Paint me, mammee," he used to say; "paint me in boo and wed stweaks and make me pooty."

And then this venerable and dignified mother would get down on the floor with her paint box, and, laughing at the various devices suggested by her imagination, would paint his fair, fat little body in all the colors of the rainbow; often streaking one leg in rings and the other in perpendicular bars or long spirals. This afforded her endless amusement, this and a hundred other little ideas, so that her girlish laugh was not long silent in the house.

It was no rare thing for me in my frequent visits to find Charley in the condition described. I made it my first business in such a case to wash him all over, and compel him to submit to the tyranny of clothes, even if I had to slap him a very little in order to accomplish my purpose. So it came about that he looked up to me and respected me out of all proportion to the respect he had for any one else. He took very little notice of his father at all, but his mother was his chief playmate. She sang hundreds of songs to him and to me as well—Scotch, German, English and Irish ballads; all the nursery rhymes; snatches from Moore, Campbell and Scott never yet set to music. She told us fairy stories and love stories, and when her supply gave out she made up others.

If it chanced that I was away for several days I always found Charley on my return complete "cock of the walk," and ruling things with a high hand. Sometimes I was a little discouraged with him, and wondered if he would ever get a sufficient sense of decency to wear his clothes. One day I had him dressed up right prettily and took him to the store, where father gave him a straw hat with a green ribbon around the crown. He was quite proud of it for a short time, and then abandoned it.

About this time one of our town ladies called on Mrs. Dalton, taking her two little daughters with her. These children were dressed very showily; and poor little Charley stood there entirely naked, looking at them admiringly and probably somewhat enviously.

He felt that his appearance was not up to the prevailing style. Breaking the spell of absorption into which his admiration of the children had drawn him, he looked at his mother and said piteously, "Where's my hat, mammee?"

I suppose some will wonder what good my association with this family could possibly do me. In the first place their influence on me was refining. In the second place they had books and knew a good deal of the best kind of literature, and were not entirely ignorant of science. But the great thing was that their helplessness called for my strength, and it responded in greater quantities than I imagined possible. It was a matter of pride with me to know that I was so necessary to them. I grew more capable; I learned to sew and cut garments with considerable dexterity. I came to making Mrs. Dalton's dresses so that she looked lovely in them; and when the doctor's father sent them money to come to Louisville and make him a visit I made a cloak and hat for her.

I was foolish enough to entrust her to select the material; and what she bought was dark blue goods with a white stripe in it.

"It won't do," I said. "That white stripe makes it unsuitable."

"Oh! well then we can paint it out," was her suggestion. And we did. We painted the stripe the same color as the body of the goods, and made it up into a long, warm cloak that did not look bad on her at all.

We spent a great deal of time over the paint box and brushes, and I was supposed to take lessons, but we only played and talked. I can see the little group now. Charley in a high chair and his mother decorating him. Sometimes she painted a wasp on his arm, so natural that he was afraid of it. Again it was a humming bird perched on one of his fat little shoulders, or, rather, hovering about it, so consummate was the skill with which she worked out her design. My baby sister and I were at the same table, both engrossed in the proceedings, no matter what they were.

"Make a 'nake, Henny," was my little sister's most frequent order. I made a snake by twisting a piece of india rubber into a close snarl and leaving it to uncurl itself.

And where was the education I was getting out of all this?

It was coming to me in many ways. It was not alone what was said and done, but what was unsaid and undone that was teaching me. Instead of being thought for, as in my own family, here I was forced to think for others. The helplessness of these people gave me strength and push and a sort of common-sense business courage that stands me in hand even yet. Besides this I learned to cut garments and make them with great skill, and this afterwards made me very useful in my own family. As there was no milliner in the place, I made pretty hats for the family out of drawn muslins and silks. These hats at that early stage were a kind of cross between hats and bonnets; but they were lovely, or, at least, we thought so then. I am sure I had naturally fine artistic tastes, and was a great lover of the beautiful; but these tastes were improved and developed by contact with the Daltons. Moreover an element of refinement pervaded their conversation and manners, and I was not slow in being impressed by it, until, as I began to enter the region of young ladyhood it was said of me by the few persons in Fairfield, competent of judging, that Helen was a "perfect lady" in her manners, and that all of Lib Wilmans' children were "very pretty behaved indeed."

To be called a lady-like girl in those days was great praise. From what I now gather in my contact with young ladies of this time I think perhaps this would be considered a very old-fashioned idea. Then, too, we were taught how to entertain our guests; also that a knowledge of standard authors was essential to our social position.

The intelligence of the place had greatly improved as I approached womanhood, and we young girls began to take pride in our culture and elegance of demeanor. I remember once when aunt Mary was home from school for a few weeks she taught me how to enter a room gracefully. The only secret of it was coming in slowly. She said a certain slowness of motion gave the appearance, if not the reality, of being at ease. Previous to this—in my embarrassment—I had come into a room where there was company with about as much grace as a cow, almost upsetting the furniture by my ungainly velocity. And after I was in and seated I did not know what to do with myself, especially my hands. Aunt Mary changed all this. "Come in with quiet dignity," was her direction, "sit down on a chair sidewise; let one hand hang over its back while the other rests in your lap, palm uppermost. And don't be ashamed of your hands, because—except my own—they are the prettiest pair in southern Illinois." And so they were at that time; but twenty-five years of cooking and dishwashing ruined their beauty afterwards.

CHAPTER VIII.

LLOYD, BILLY WILKES AND SALLY START A CIRCUS.

About this time aunt Mary taught me how to entertain company. Our little town was quite gay, and we gave and attended parties frequently.

When the party was at our house, aunt Mary said I had no right to indulge myself by talking to the pleasantest people in the rooms. On the contrary I must seek out the retiring and bashful and neglected ones and unite them in conversation with the others, making them feel at ease; thus giving them all the pleasure I could. She said it made no difference whether I had a good time or not; my only interest was to see that my guests were happy.

I suppose all this is very old-fashioned stuff now, but at that time our reputations were built on what we believed to be good manners, together with a certain knowledge of books.

I think I had quite a good understanding of the word "lady," and I desired most earnestly to fill my conception of it. Even then I knew that mere external training could not make any one a lady, but that the true quality had its roots deep down in a fine, just nature. To be a true lady is to be filled with beautiful conceptions of kindness and sweetness, and to permit these conceptions to shine through the body and permeate the actions. I do not pretend to say that I was all this, but simply that I desired to be it, and that I probably actualized my desire in some slight degree.

I have dwelt very little upon the growth of the religious idea in my mind in these later chapters, but it was there all the time, though obscured by Mrs. Dalton's influence. Not that she influenced me against it; she never seemed to think of it at all, and it was not talked of between us. She simply interested me in other things. It was only at home that I was under the cloud of the fear of hell and a vengeful God.

Aunt Mary had accepted religion in her characteristic way. She did not doubt its claims at all. She believed in hell and a vengeful God, and thought they were needed for other people, but not for herself. She knew these terrors were not for her; she was quite sure of her own salvation; she believed that her absence from heaven would render that charming abode incomplete. At least this is the way I think she felt, and I am sure she never had any uneasiness on the subject. She said she intended to join the church when she got too old to dance, but not before.

This settled matters so far as she was concerned, but it left me in the same wretched condition. Mother had quit dancing, and what dancing I was doing was done under the flagellation of an accusing conscience.

All this time I was not only carrying the burden of my own sins, but of my brothers and sisters as well. Sometimes I would begin to let my reason operate, and then would catch a glimpse of the fact that none of us were particularly sinful. Indeed, we were good children, and harmonious and loving and generous, and gave mother very little trouble. But I did not dare follow out any such line of thought as this. It was treason to God, who said that all were sinners—every one.

Many and many a night when I would start out in my thought to discover what sins I had committed, and could find none, I would be sorely nonplused. But I always fell back on the assumption that God knew, and God said we were all sinners. Then the cloud deepened and my heart weakened until it felt like lead within me. I am sure that in this one thing

I laid the foundation of that which made me a physical wreck later in life.

This weakening of my heart broke up my splendid circulation in time, impaired my perfect digestion so that every vital organ was underfed, and the whole body began to break down. These results were slow in coming, however, and I was a middle-aged woman before I began to feel their full force.

I dread the writing of these chapters that have anything to do with my religious experiences. I must live over the same experiences in writing them, and I have a horror of them. I really have a greater horror of them now as I review them from my present standpoint than I had in going through them. I did not fully comprehend how death-dealing they were to the vital principle at that time. I simply suffered in a dumb way, but without knowing the extent of the ruin that was being wrought in my splendid physical organization. I see now what profanation the religion of the age is; I see how it kills as it goes, thus working out its own deadly scheme inch by inch. I did not see it then. My brain had not ripened to the power of such perception; so I simply suffered dumbly as an animal might suffer from some dull, slow torture it could not get away from.

If I relate this part of my life in a fragmentary manner the reader will understand the reason. I was naturally a happy disposition. I was interested in everything and could extract happiness from each passing event. Trifles were not trifles to me. They had meaning. I lived deep down in the heart of nature and was content simply to live and grow. And this condition—which is one of perfect health—was poisoned by the infamous theological rot that pervaded the entire mental atmosphere of that time. Let me drop the subject for a while. I shall have to come back to it oftener than I want to, and oftener than my readers will want me to.

I have not done with my childhood yet. I still extract merriment out of my recollection of the experiences I had with my brothers and sisters in the old log house so long ago. The house had grown to be an eight-room structure, and was weather boarded over the logs, and painted white. It had big verandas and was comfortable, and—for that place—quite elegant.

I suppose most people would look upon our old town as the deadest place imaginable; but we did not seem to lack for excitement. Everybody knew everybody's business, and gossip was more wildly interesting than the theatre going of a later and deader time.

Nobody was more interested in the town gossip than
I was. I was too eagerly alive not to want to know
all that was passing. I have an idea that people must
be very dead indeed before they cease to be interested
in the affairs of their neighbors. I have not lost this
interest yet, and never expect to. I think that I have
been too much interested in them and that it has been
a source of unhappiness. I have borne their burdens
to my own grief, not knowing that burden bearing
is a foolish thing either for myself or others. People
of wide sympathies flow out into other lives, depleting
themselves and doing the others no good.

I still feel this same outflowing, but it carries a
healthier thought than that of pity. It is now the
bearer of courage and of the strength that conquers.

Of course, everybody knew everybody else in Fairfield. If a covered wagon stopped in the place long
enough to water the jaded horses at the old well with
the creaking windlass and the "moss-covered bucket,"
a crowd of men and childfen gathered about it immediately. While the men were questioning the
owner of the team, we youngsters would be gazing on
the many tow heads protruding from under the wagon
sheet. A silent scrutiny, long protracted, was all that
usually came of these interviews. Only once do I

remember being spoken to, and for years I retained the remembrance of that little girl as a creature too bold to be countenanced by other members of her sex. I saw nothing but her head with its unkempt hair; her eyes were bright and round and alert; she looked like a squirrel, and I still have an undefined impression that there was a little brown curly tail raised over her back, if only one could have seen through the canvas top that hid her body. After looking at me with a wide-awake, irresponsible expression for a few moments, she said, "My name's Roxy Mariar Turnipseed; what's yourn?"

I think I jumped nervously. I did so mentally if not physically. I was so stupefied by her boldness in speaking at all that I overlooked for the moment the strangeness of her name. I made no answer, not because I did not want to, but because I had nothing to say. I was a timid child and could not—all of a sudden—address a stranger. Seeing that I did not answer, her round eyes began to gather a mighty intent, and her nerveless little face became rigid and brusque.

"You're proud," she said. "You think you're mighty fine, dressed up in a white frock. I got one myself in ma's chist, but I won't war it everyday.

I'm too keerful of it for that. I don't believe in gals as wars their best clothes week days. Then they haint got nothin' for Sunday."

A long pause, and then, "*You* haint got no year bobs, (ear rings) and I hev."

As the wagon rolled along the street I could see the little self-assertive face all puckered into dauntless resolve to crush my pride, until a corner was turned and it was gone. And there I stood helpless, when I might have told her that my father kept store, and that my mother had a silk dress, and that we had a lovely carriage with a pair of horses that were big and fat and handsome, and that I had a real gold chain and locket. Imagine the bitterness of my regret under such circumstances. The only comfort I took to myself whenever I reviewed the event, as I frequently did, was to decide very emphatically that she did not know anything about ladylike manners, and that she was so ignorant she mispronounced her words; but above all that she was bold, whereas the beauty of a girl was modesty, and not to speak until she is spoken to. I must admit that this was very indifferent satisfaction, and did not at all supersede my desire to "use her up" with the most cruelly cutting sarcasm; but it was my only resource.

Mother was a woman of immense vitality. I am sure of it simply by recalling her laugh, though I have many other evidences of the fact. She was the right material for making a famous woman in more ways than one, but the time in which she lived was against her development. I fear I have created the impression that she was ill-natured. Nothing could be farther from the truth.

I never saw such diversity of capacity in one person. There seemed to be nothing she could not plan out, and then hold in reserve the vitality for executing it. And her laugh! Such a variety of things as it expressed! It was as intelligent as the speech of most persons. It was now kindly and encouraging, and now sympathetic, and then satirical; always full of meaning. She was fond of her children and proud of them. She was probably very much more indulgent than I had any idea of at the time. No doubt she held us in check sufficiently to make us feel that the reins were there, and that it was no use to pull very far in a forbidden direction.

One evening the clouds closed down darkly. It was going to storm. Mother got us all in and ran her bright, sunshiny eyes over us, taking a mental census no doubt.

"Where's Lloyd?" she asked.

"Should think you'd know 'thout askin'," said Ivens.

"Is he with that Wilkes boy again?"

"Yes, ma'm, he is; and him and Billy Wilkes is gettin' ready to run off, cos both of 'em won't stand things much longer; choppin' wood and bein' tied to the wood pile, and bringin' in chips and carryin' slops to the pigs, an' doin' lots of things; an' I don't blame 'em. I couldn't stan' it myself, but my sperit's broke."

The fat thing that made this rather startling announcement was sitting on both his bare feet in a chair. His round black eyes shone like two diamonds with health and vitality; his cheeks were like russet apples in which the rich carmine is struggling through the soft bronze; his pretty red mouth was pouched out, and his double chin formed a cradle, wherein his real chin—the one with a dimple in it—rested peacefully. As he spoke, other little reproachful dimples appeared and withdrew again; and then repose.

Father was present. He looked at this youngster whose "sperit was broke;" the dancing light in his eyes gloomed over with sudden solemnity, and he turned his head away.

"Lloyd's a bad boy," said mother, but with a laugh that cancelled the meaning of her words. It was a laugh full of pride for this precocious little imp, and for the other one who sat there defending him. Father caught the meaning of her laugh, and there rose before him a vision of his absent son; a comprehensive vision that covered his whole life from the moment the nurse laid the fair twelve-pound baby in his arms, down to the morning of the present day, when—as he phrased it—he had "got away with the whole family in a general blow up"; this "blow up" evidently being the excuse for the projected run away.

Father sat forward, bolt upright, in his chair, and smilingly, scratched his head.

"It," he said, meaning Lloyd; "do you remember, Lib, when we went to Graysville to see William and Caroline, how the little devil would stand up in the carriage all the time, and how he fought you for trying to hold him? He wouldn't even let you touch his dress on the sly; he kept looking round and snatching it out of your hands, till pretty soon the carriage took a bump and stood still, and out he pitched into dust a foot deep."

"And it's fortunate the dust was so deep," said mother. "But wasn't he a pickle when you took him up?"

"And do you remember after that, how you couldn't

hold him tight enough to satisfy him? But wasn't he scared? 'Twas the richest thing I ever saw. That was the day he called you an old sinner. 'Hold me, mamma,' he said; 'now, mamma, take hold o' me dwess,' and he gathered up a little piece of his dress and crowded it into your hand. 'Now, if oo let do o' me, mamma, me'll be awfy mad. Me don't want to fall out adain.'"

"Yes," said mother, "and being as he had tormented the life out of me before he fell out, I thought I would torment him a little afterwards. So I pretended to be very indifferent, and would let his dress slide through my fingers, till he got so worked up he gave me a piece of his mind. 'You mean old tinner,' he said. 'Me'll trade oo off and dit anudder mamma. Where did me dit oo anyhow?' 'I expect the Lord gave me to you,' said I. 'I wish he hadn't a done it,' said he, as quick as a flash, flinging a look backwards over his little polished white shoulder, 'I wish he hadn't a done it; and he wouldn't needer, only you're so mean he didn't want you hisself.'"

Father laughed hilariously. "He got away with you there, Lib," he said; "fact is, he's been getting away with all of us ever since. But wasn't he the prettiest baby that ever lived?"

At this there was a perfect babble of voices going up in protest. It was, "You said I was the prettiest," and "you said *I* was the prettiest." Even the boy whose "sperit was broke" forgot his calamitous condition to say, "Papa, you said I was the prettiest;" while little Emma pressed close to his knee, putting in her claims with her dove-like eyes, even though her cupid's bow of a mouth opened not.

"You were all the prettiest," said he kindly, "each in his or her turn."

Presently Lloyd made his appearance, coming in with a gust of wind. His hair was all tousled up, and his blue eyes were wide open. He was afraid of a storm, and the storm was on us. He sat down sulkily and pulled his hat over his eyes. We children began to ask him about his contemplated trip, but he made no answer. To our surprise neither father nor mother had a word to say about it, and were evidently at rest in their minds, and I believe I may say that they were rather unusually cheerful in their talk. This surprised me as I knew that Lloyd's escapades had given them both no less trouble than they had given me.

The truth is, mother and Mrs. Wilkes had entered into a conspiracy. They were not going to frustrate—

openly—any attempt of their naughty boys to run away. They would try other means.

The next day Lloyd made up quite a bundle of clothes and provisions, nobody opposing him, and carried them over to Mrs. Wilkes' wood pile, where Billy Wilkes was to meet him with a similar bundle.

Now, Billy had a little sister Sally who worshiped him, and who bore all of his snubs with great fortitude, never questioning his right to say what he pleased to her; and Mrs. Wilkes told us later how this little thing followed him everywhere while he was making his preparations to leave. So, watching this wonderful brother, she became convinced that running away was a great performance, and the one thing desirable above all other things. Presently she informed him that she was "doin' to wun off too."

"Lawful sakes! You!" said he contemptuously, straightening himself up and looking like a prince of the blood in this young lady's eyes; "why, you're a baby. You ain't got sense enough to take care of yourself yet."

Sally was deeply abashed by this announcement, but rallied a little later, and asked meekly:

"Tant oo take care of me, Billy?"

This was putting a new face on the matter. Billy

thought perhaps he could. So Sally began to make up a bundle for herself. She went to the dirty clothes basket, and got one of her mother's kitchen aprons and a towel. These she pinned together in one of the most demoralized packages ever seen. She exhausted the pin cushion in disposing of its stray ends, and even then the result was shaky and uncertain, besides being so "stickery," she was afraid to handle it. Mrs. Wilkes found it the next day at the wood pile, and chuckling with merriment she brought it over and showed it to mother and the rest of us.

When these two babies had joined the other baby— Lloyd—waiting outside, there arose a dispute about the propriety of taking Sally. Lloyd told Billy quite plainly that he did not propose working to help support her.

"Yes," said Billy, "but don't you see her'll help us more'n all the dorgs and the pigs throwed in? Her'll be better'n a Shetland pony. Her can dance and sing a song and make two speeches; her's just what we want for our circus. Should think you'd have gumption enough to see that for yourself. 'Sides that, she's the prettiest little girl in the world."

Lloyd seemed doubtful of Sally's accomplishments; so Billy proposed to put her through her "paces" and show him what she could do. Sally by this time began to see that she was going to star it in a travelling circus, and became wildly elated. She sang her song in such a joyous, caroling, sweet little voice she really would have brought down the house in the best theatre in the world. But, as often happens with superlative genius, her pearls were cast before swine. Lloyd gave a sniff of contempt.

"Her can't talk plain," he said; "her's nothin' but a baby."

The tears came into her eyes, but her lordly brother ordered her to "dry up and cut loose in a dance." So she brushed her tears away, and, beginning a little tune, she kept step to it very accurately, beating time by clapping her hands together. This was so pretty and graceful that even Lloyd applauded. Then Billy ordered her to "come on" with her speeches. The first of these was from "Mother Goose." The emphasis with which she delivered it was quite inimitable, and only a feeble attempt at its expression can be conveyed on paper. She stepped out before her audience with her curly head well up and her whole bearing proud as a peacock (I know, because I was watching, together with Mrs. Wilkes, from a hole in the kitchen where the "chinking" was badly broken);

then she began with her exquisite baby lisp, not to be rendered in type:

"Hokey pokey, hanky panky,
I'm the queen of Swinkey Swankey,
And I'm pretty well I thank'ee."

At the last word she swept them a courtesy like a real queen, and retired modestly backward waiting for another call.

Lloyd did not approve of the speech. The same criticism with which he condemned the song was in force here. But the dance was "bully" he said, so he thought they would take her. Then they revealed their plans. They had three dogs and a pig, and Sally, and were starting out for a "show." They were going to work their way to New York, where they intended to stop and live in a house with gold floors and diamond windows, and have all the fine things they wanted, and go riding on Shetland ponies every day.

It was now getting on toward the middle of the afternoon, and they declared themselves ready to start. At this juncture Mrs. Wilkes thought I had better go out and urge them to stay until after dinner.

But no, they did not care for dinner; they had plenty with them, and when that gave out they would have a show and buy more.

"Ah! yes," said I—having been primed by Mrs. Wilkes—"but we are going to have a pie, and a cake with raisins in it as big as your thumb. What do you think of that?"

Their eyes dilated. "That's bully," Lloyd said. So they held a consultation and decided to wait until after dinner. As they sat on the wood pile pending that pleasant event, the time seemed interminable to them; and it was a very long hour, indeed, before they were called in.

After dinner the sun hung so low in the west they held another conference about starting, the result of which was that they would camp out in a broken-down wagon on the edge of town, while Sally remained in the house that night, where they could call for her in the morning and take an early start. They had a long walk to the wagon, and when they got there were almost surprised and deeply injured to find no sleeping accommodations; not that they had calculated on sleeping accommodations, but simply that they had not calculated at all—and the gas was beginning to leak out of their inflated ideal.

After a little thinking they stole an old horse blanket out of a barn not far away. Then they remembered their three dogs and one pig tied up with bale rope clear out on the other side of the village, and it came into their heads that these stock actors might be hungry. The next thing in order was to feed them. They had almost reached the place where they had left them when they happened to think that they had brought no food. Here was an emergency. They were growing discouraged. It was getting dark. In a dumb way they were beginning to realize the total depravity of inanimate things. Finally, as it must be done, they retraced their steps to get the bread and meat out of their bundles.

They had reached the growling stage of fatigue, and went along saying naughty words such as "durn" and "dogon," and "I golly," and it was reported that one of them said "damn," but they both denied this afterwards to their mothers.

"What are we goin' to do for bread now?" asked Billy.

"I can get more at home," said Lloyd.

"It's goin' to be a devil of a trip, this is," said Billy. "I'm nearly tired to death now."

But they trudged on and got their provisions, and returned with them to the spot where their hungry dependents had been stationed. Here they were surprised and disgusted to find the dogs gone. The renegades had not had the charity to liberate their cousin in bonds, for he was still there sitting back on his tether with the obstinacy of a—of a pig. That there was blood on the moon for him that night was betrayed by the wicked expression of his eye. Still he did not refuse the food; he ate it to the last bite, and then watched them reproachfully and ungratefully.

By this time it was quite dark, and they had a good half mile to travel back to the wagon. They now took each other by the hand for protection and scampered rapidly away.

They did not undress that night; and so strong is the force of habit they did not know how to go to bed without undressing, especially as they had no bed to go to. Even after they were in the wagon they could not sleep, but lay staring in the dark for many hours, as they supposed.

The time—in reality—was not so long as they imagined. They were nervous and restless, preternaturally alive to every sound that moved the leaves and every sigh of the night wind. But after a while as they listened in this state of intensity, they heard an unmistakable groan under the wagon. With a simultaneous movement they popped the blanket over their heads where they had to hold it by main force, so great was the capillary attraction that impelled it upwards; and then they heard another groan. This time it was simply awful. It began with the true graveyard sound, but was worse and more of it, ending in a double demi-semi-quaver of explosive volume that might have resembled the bursting of a long withheld laugh but for the horror of it. Anything so demoniacal was never heard in that town before. It almost shook the planks in the bottom of their bed room, and tore its way up through the cracks; the blanket over them gave them an idea that they were bottled in with this ghastly terror. This was not to be endured for an instant; and so, with another simultaneous impulse, or, to avoid tautology, let us say with two impulses that were Siamese twins in their kinship, they sprang over the side of the wagon and ran for their lives.

There was no holding each other now. It was "every fellow for himself, and the devil take the hindmost." Billy was ahead. Lloyd's roars were unheeded, and gradually died out in the distance. He said, later in life, that one of his legs fainted and left him nothing to travel on but the other leg and his head, with a little assistance from his elbows, which were in a half fainting condition also. He never could recall where his hands were. When he reached home he found us still up. His appearance among us was decidedly tumultuous. He took his seat quietly, and to the questions, "What you been doin' Lloyd? What makes you look so pale?" he answered but one word.

"Nothin'."

The next morning when Sally opened her blue eyes (so Mrs. Wilkes reported) she screamed lustily for that mighty man Billy. When he came she informed him that she was ready to start; and great was her wonder when he told her to "shut up and not bother him about such nonsense any more."

CHAPTER IX.

THE STORY OF TEN LITTLE HATS.

How the Daltons disappeared from my life I cannot tell. It seems strange that we can remember things so perfectly up to a certain point, and then absolute darkness rest upon the remainder.

I have an idea that they never returned from Louisville after the doctor's father sent for them. But fate kept weaving and weaving and weaving for all of us, and I met them again many years after in California. But they no longer awakened the interest in me they had done in my childhood. The doctor had taken to drink. Mrs. Dalton had a heart-broken look, and seemed as helpless as a baby in her own house, keeping it dirty and wretched beyond description. Charley had passed from the extreme of wearing no clothes to the other extreme of wearing very fine ones. But I have nothing to say against Charley. He was the best electrician in the state, and was employed at a splendid salary. He supported the family; but what a family it was to support!

The money he gave them was like water poured in a rat hole. It made no show whatever.

The doctor died of drink. Mrs. Dalton told me she had nothing to live for but Charley. In less than a year Charley died. After this I dreaded to meet her, but I did meet her. She made no sign of grief as I had feared. Her face was as impassive as stone, and as gray. The poor little thing was really dead then. One morning she did not get up. It was all over except the burial, which followed immediately.

What a comment on life in its present stage of development the history of this gifted creature is! How lovely it would have been if I could have held her for an indefinite period in all the charm of her early womanhood as she appeared to me then! The evanescence of these sweet, bright lives is the most pitiful thing I know. It was sorrows like this that started me to thinking of possibilities far beyond the ordinary thoughts of the age and race. Of these thoughts I shall speak later.

As this personal narrative unwinds itself I feel like loitering. I see that I am being carried out of the region, and beyond the experiences of childhood, and I do not like it. There is so much in the child—to one who has anything like a true conception of him—that to pass out of the circle of his life into the arid zone of manhood, which is the grave rather than the fruitage of his early possibilities, is like abandoning a mine in which lies concealed the never-to-be-revealed wealth that might redeem a whole world.

Children are so wonderful in their simple naturalness. It seems as if the growing power of the earth—that power which produces flowers and fruit and all life and beauty out of hidden depths—is in them, and speaks through them in all their little sweet, innocent ways.

To leave home with a circus—if I remember correctly—was Lloyd's last effort to break from parental authority. All of these attempts occurred within quite a short space of time. I think the whole series did not occupy more than a year or two. But there is one of them that I have omitted to tell about. I think it came in just after the failure of the young man's circus business, in which Sally was to star it over the country as the chief attraction. It was an effort that might have proved disastrous, but did not, in consequence of that ubiquitous law which seems to exist solely for the benefit of such youngsters. Having evolved his plan, he kept quiet about it until circumstances favored him in executing it. One Saturday when the town was full of half-drunken men, and great excitement prevailed, his time came. He saw a mettlesome, high-spirited horse, all equipped for riding, tied to a neighboring fence.

"I'll get on it and ride it to New York right off when nobody aint a lookin'; cos what's the use of waitin'?" he said.

And he did get on. However, things did not work as he planned.

Mother was ironing. Lloyd came in, climbed up on the far corner of the table and sat very still indeed. Presently his quietness attracted her attention. Quietness in boys is very apt to arouse parental anxiety.

"What's the matter?" mother asked.

"Nothin'."

"Are you sick?"

"No'm."

"What makes you so pale?"

"Nothin'."

"Do you want a piece of cake?"

"No—yes, if it's got raisins in it."

The cake was produced, but his appetite was not so sharp as usual.

"What have you been up to?" asked mother.

"Nothin'."

"Where have you been?"

"Nowhere."

"I'll bet a thousand dollars you've been hatching mischief, if a body could only find it out. Tell me, now, haven't you?"

"Haven't I what?"

"What have you been doing?"

"Nothin'."

"Tell me immediately where you have been."

"Aint been nowhere."

At this moment there was a tumult on the front porch. Two or three men rushed in. "Where's Lloyd?" they cried in a breath.

Then they saw him and explained. He had climbed on one of the most dangerous horses in the county, they said, and it had run off with him, kicking and plunging awfully. Several men had mounted other horses standing around and given chase. They had overtaken the horse and brought it back, but could find no trace of Lloyd. Half the town was out now looking for his remains, and the greatest consternation prevailed.

"Where did he throw you, Lloyd?" was asked.

"Who throw me?" said Lloyd.

"The horse; where did the horse throw you?"

"Wot horse?"

"The horse you got on round by Dingley's saloon."

"Didn't get on no horse."

"You must be mistaken," said mother to the men. "Is it possible that it was some other boy?" queried one.

Lloyd munched his cake silently. More people were coming. All of them questioned him. Many went away doubting; others felt certain their eyes had not deceived them. Pretty soon the schoolmaster arrived. He was deeply versed in the hidden ways of boys. A life time spent in ferreting out the crooked paths and dark mysteries of this labyrinthine institution, aided by recollections of his own boyhood, had made him almost omniscient with regard to them. He asked no questions. He walked about the floor talking to mother on all manner of subjects except *the* subject. Lloyd began to feel neglected. At last the subject under discussion was horsemanship. The schoolmaster it seemed was a good rider; had performed wonderful equestrian feats in his boyhood and passed many a hair-breadth escape.

"Thinks he's the only feller in the world that dares ride," thought Lloyd.

"Now," said the schoolmaster, "the boy that rode that horse to-day knew nothing at all of the science of riding. To be sure, I didn't see him as he rode through the town, but I am informed on good authority that he was actually frightened almost to death, so that his hair stood on end."

Lloyd raised one little paw and smoothed his hair down.

"And his tongue clove to the roof of his mouth."

Lloyd put out his tongue and felt it.

"And that, instead of pulling on the reins as a brave boy would, he dropped them and clung to the horn of the saddle like grim death. I wonder if that could be possible; if the boy did actually drop the reins like a coward, and—

"No," said Lloyd, "you can bet your last quarter that's a lie. I pulled on him hard enough to break his durned neck, and he wouldn't stop."

Mother looked at the school teacher, and he looked at her; then they both looked at Lloyd. He sat on one corner of the table with his knees drawn up and his hands clasped around them. He might have been covered with a good sized water bucket, and there he was saying, "I pulled on him hard enough to break his durned neck, and he wouldn't stop."

It was too comical. Mother laughed one of her most meaning laughs; the teacher's dry chuckle made strange contrast with its musicalness. Everybody in the room laughed. "Oh! if his father was only here," said mother; "what would I give if Caleb could see him now?"

"Did the horse know you was on him, Lloyd?" asked Ivens.

"If he didn't know more than you do, he didn't know nothin'," was the brotherly rejoinder.

What unflagging pertinacity these young folks have. Parents may resolve and re-resolve; but *they* only resolve once; *they* hang unchanging to the same resolution while dynasties vanish and systems wax and wane—so to speak; *they* never let up; the mother's resistance wears threadbare in places; *they* perceive the weakening, and with that vitality which knows no need of rest they walk in and have their own way at last.

Nine times out of ten the mother has this almost ungovernable vital force to contend with entirely unaided by the father of the flock, and she breaks down under it. This was the case with us, and I have observed the same thing in other families. Men refuse to share this responsibility with their wives, and they in turn become the victims of the perpetual and undirected force of the children. Here is an experience illustrative of the fact.

Scene in front of a neat cottage. A gentleman

comes through the gate. A very small person slips out under his arm, and they stand face to face on the sidewalk. Gentleman glances weakly towards the house, and calls, "Mamma!"

There is the flutter of a white frock on the porch, and a voice from behind the vines.

"Well, what now?"

"Tootsie's got out."

Concealed voice—"Oh! come off with your helplessness; why don't you put her back?"

Weak-kneed Papa—"Go back in the house, Tootsie, and I'll bring you some candy."

Tootsie—"Me yont do it."

W. K. P.—"Where you going?"

Tootsie—"Me doin' wiz oo."

W. K. P.—"But I'm going down town on the car."

Tootsie—"I doin' on ee tar too."

W. K. P.: (In a quavering voice.) "Mamma!" (A little stronger.) "Oh, Ma! My God! what shall I do? Kate! Kate! I wish I may never tell the truth again if she hasn't gone in and shut the door. Well, blankety-blank the pertinacity of a baby anyhow! See here, Toots, I'll tell you what; you can come with me as far as the green trees, and then you can run home again, and papa'll go down town."

Tootsie—"Me aint doin' to do it. Me's doin' down town too."

W. K. P.—(Another hope of rescue animating his soul, casts his eyes towards the rear of the house and sees a servant; straightens himself up into his most commanding attitude, and gives directions for carrying the rebel in doors.)

In the anarchistic melee that ensues he makes his escape, but without one thought as to how the vitality of this pretty little creature can be directed into ways that will make a heaven of the home where it abides, and whose beneficence will reach so far beyond the home as to become a special guard against the poverty and distress that assail so many families in whom this mighty power is suffered to go to waste, or, worse still, to become a destructive element to itself and others.

Much thought on this subject has led me to the conclusion that there are scarcely any parents who have sense enough to raise their own children. Moreover, the system of isolated households is not conducive to the highest development of these gifted little creatures, who possess along with their brains the natural push, the inherent vitality, to lift this old world out of the ruts of dogmatic thought, in which it has been stranded for ages, and send it spinning into a perfect wonderland of new and great ideas and hopes, all capable of being harnessed to the practical needs of our coming humanity.

But where are Billy Wilkes and Sally and Lloyd? Am I too old to write the history of these bright young creatures? Really it seems so since I have survived the best of them. But Billy still lives. He is a rich man and a hard one. He scarcely allowed his faithful mother enough to gratify her hunger in her lonely old age. He turned his back on Sally all through the years of her greatest need. I do not know whether he is a happy man or not, for I cannot tell what conditions a man of his character requires for happiness.

Sally's lot was the lot of many another woman. She married and brought children into the world and lived in anxiety, pain and poverty, unappreciated and mentally alone. For she was a gifted girl who, as a crushed wife, found no outlet for the best part of her. She was a body slave to her husband—day and night—a man never worthy of even blacking her boots. She clung to life for her children alone, and died when they seemed to need her most.

But Lloyd. I was in California when he wrote me

that he had joined the army. The news almost took the breath out of me; for I am not a sufficiently loyal citizen to gird the sword to the bodies of my loved ones, as the Spartan mothers did, and bid them go forth to conquest. I looked upon war as legalized murder, and thought that those who believed in it ought to do the fighting. I was not then, and am not now, actuated by any false ideas of glory as connected with the matter. I wrote the boy—just verging into promising and beautiful manhood—to get out of it as soon as he could. Months passed and I heard nothing. I never heard form him again except indirectly. He was one of the victims of the Fort Andersonville horror. It was there that his magnificent young life perished inch by inch under the unspeakable cruelty of the system of starvation practiced upon the Northern soldiers by their Southern captors.

The lady who reads these chapters in proof, before they are made into plates for electrotyping, has a little daughter; and this daughter has little friends, all of whom want to hear every word of "A Search for Freedom." When the proof sheets come from Boston there is quite a ripple of excitement. They really think I am writing a child's story.

But it hurts them fearfully when one of my characters dies. That the death of Lloyd and Sally should be allowed to finish a chapter was more than they could bear. They think I ought to tell the story of the "Ten little hats" right here in this place to make my readers "so's they'll quit feeling bad before they lay down the paper." There is nothing in this story of the hats; and I have no idea that it will appear as well in print as when I do it in pantomime for the small "tousle pates" who are now putting their compulsion on me. But here it is:

Not long ago I attended a Chautauqua in the delusive hope of learning something. I had not then found out that these places were run in the interests of religion. I was finding it out, however, pretty fast. I was on an elevated seat overlooking the ground floor, on which was grouped a number of splint bottomed chairs, placed there probably for the convenience of the deaf and old and otherwise decrepit part of the population. I was waiting for the lecture to begin. My hopes concerning the lecture were not enthusiastic since discovering that the whole affair was conducted on the principle of a grown up Sunday school; for if there was anything on earth I was born hating, and had been true to my feelings for it first, last and all the time, it was that institution. As I sat there waiting I let my mind run back in the past until it came among the days whose happiness—though not unalloyed—was never very bitterly broken except by the advent of the Seventh Day. I thought of aunt Sally and her slipper; and of Brother Findlay and his "sermings," and of all the boys and girls whose presence made that period more vitally alive than any later period of my life. It is the aliveness of children that causes us to look back to childhood as the happiest time, and not really the happiness of it.

By the time I had come this far in my cogitations the drone of the speaker's voice broke in on me. It *was* a preacher. I did not need to look up and see; and as for listening, I felt sure I could find some better method of amusement. I had come to listen to a scientific lecture, and here I was; fooled again.

The seats in the meantime had been filling up somewhat, and ten little girls, children of campers on the Chautauqua grounds, came filing in. I had passed a crowd of them when I entered the pavilion, and now they had come to hear the lecture. They were from four to seven years old; they all had on broad-brimmed sun hats, and as they passed by the benches and took seats in the splint chairs I could not see their faces, and not much of their forms; about all I saw was their hats.

Ten little girls all in a row; ten pair of heels hitched upon the rungs of ten chairs; ten intelligent looking hats tilted at an angle which proved that they were taking a critical survey of the preacher.

Those expressive ten hats were evidently gauging him to see if there was anything in him likely to "pan out" for their entertainment.

Something took my attention away from them for a short time, and when I looked again they had shifted their position by bringing the chairs into a circle, and the hats were tipped down in front as if the owners were contemplating the toes of their pretty shoes.

Presently one hat quivered, and came to a level; then nine other hats came to the same level, and I knew that ten pair of bright eyes were looking into each other, though I could not see them.

Again my attention wandered; when I got round to the hats once more, after an absence of only a few minutes, they were all huddled together, and there was little to be seen except the backs and almost emptied seats of the ten splint chairs. Some evidently profound caucus was in active progress under the hats, as I knew by the more than auricular movement of the broad brims.

For the brims dipped and came up again in a manner so positive as to defy opposition; then they quivered—with emotion probably; and pretty soon one of them, the leading hat, perhaps, rocked from side to side as if it had put in a clincher that no other hat could stand up against.

Some of the hats giggled; it is a positive fact. To use our expressive Yankee dialect, they "snickered right eout." Not that they made any noise; they did not; and yet they laughed violently. I saw them do it with my own eyes. Besides that, laughing is catching, and a row of older hats not far away caught it.

And worse still, while some of my neighbors were aghast at the awfulness of this performance, and wondering where these dreadful children would go to when they died, I saw one hat tumble back convulsively while a small pair of feet appeared among the conclave of remaining hats, where they gyrated wildly.

Here the preacher paused ominously, and took a steady look at the hats; upon which they instantly got back to their second position. Then he went on with his discourse, whereat the hats became agitated, and after a few minutes fell into a hurried consultation from which they seemed to derive the satisfaction they were seeking.

At last it became apparent that they had forgotten the preacher, and from their wise noddings and shakings, I felt sure they were discussing previous experiences of similar hair-breadth escapes.

As the subject of hair-breadth escapes is in the direct road leading to fearful stories of spooks and hobgoblins and squeegicumsquees "wot swallers theirselves," I am sure it did so in this instance with the hats. For the hats trembled at times, and then became deadly still; occasionally one of them would whisk round spasmodically as if to see what was behind it; and then every one of the other hats would do the same thing.

And all the time the hats were getting closer together. They got so close presently that they began to impede each other's movements. In this way they became less expressive so that I lost much of the horror of the tales they were telling.

But I saw enough to give me a better idea of the character of hats than I had ever had before. It was the first time I really knew what a hat was. I had imagined it made of straw and other dead stuff. I did not know that the girls who made hats sewed their own fears and hopes and loves and wisdom—such wisdom as it is—and giggles and pouts and all the other attributes that go to make up a girl, into them; but they do.

As I observed, some pages back, I am loathe to leave the region of childhood. Children are such wonderful beginnings of totally perverted endings. As beginnings, they are so suggestive of what they might become, but which none of them have become as yet. Looking at them now I often seem to enter into their little lives with my bigger experience and—in a sense—to live for them on wiser lines than they know—as yet—how to live.

But I must say, and very emphatically too, that it is not the proper thing to try to project our own lives through the lives of children. Hands off; they are entitled to their own experiences. True knowledge is self-evolved, and is the result of the action of thought upon the mistakes we make. Leave the children in a large measure to their own mistakes. Nothing will teach them so thoroughly. Watch them carefully that they steer clear of dangerous folly, but otherwise leave them alone as much as possible. Let nature grow through them. She knows how to do it better than we do. She has power to develop them on lines unknown to the creed-warped tribe which we represent. She has not exhausted her resources in us. On the contrary, we are only the first faint prophecy of what she can do in making men and women, if left free.

It must be because children are the unadulterated germs of men and women, that I love to watch them so. After they begin to enter adulthood, and even before, the warping process commences; and as time advances the original plan appears to be forgotten. No wonder the wise man said: "Except ye become as little children ye shall not enter into the kingdom of heaven."

The kingdom of heaven is the realm of growth. It is the region of endless progression. Cease to progress and death sets in that very moment. Children represent on the unconscious plane the possibilities we have power to evolve on the conscious or intellectual plane. The secret of their fascination lies in this fact. They are the immortal Sphynx, the understanding of which means the conquest of all life's ills and the mastery of death itself.

CHAPTER X.

TWO OFFERS OF MARRIAGE.

I sometimes wonder at the glamour that disguises marriage. Young girls look forward to it as the end of all their anxieties and the beginning of eternal bliss. And yet they see their own mothers—who once believed the same thing—sunken into the very depths of drudgery and wretchedness, often without a loving word from their husbands from year's end to year's end. And even these mothers, in spite of their experience, are still under the same delusion with regard to their daughters, and look forward with what little hope they have left to marriage as the ultimatum of bliss for them. I can only account for this seeming obtuseness of intelligence on one hypothesis. That is, that life on the present plane is simply one of promises that have as yet reached no fulfillment. It is a life of embryonic happiness not developed beyond the prophetic germinal point.

I myself am beginning to be happy; and this happiness is increasing yearly; but it is a result of the higher knowledge which the study of the latent forces of mind is bringing me; a growing perception of man's ability to master his environment through the unfoldment of native thought. I can look back and see myself when I was submerged in the old belittling race beliefs, and I say emphatically. that there is no happiness in them; nothing but the germinal forecast of happiness. They form a period in race growth; the hopes they suggest—though utterly delusive on the plane of their birth—still point to a time of fulfillment on a higher plane.

The entire past has simply been the seed bearing period; the period when children are begotten to keep the world populated until such time as human intelligence has reached a point in knowledge where there will be no farther need of child bearing; but where the vital forces that now produce the child will pass up to a higher expression, and perpetuate indefinitely the lives of the individuals themselves.

It is to this plane that thousands of the foremost members of the race are now arising. But at the time I am writing of, this idea was wrapped in almost absolute darkness.

It is true that in looking back I can see the premonitions of its existence in myself. But my intellect—at that time—warped out of all semblance of individuality—had no power to interpret these premonitions; and so I permitted myself to be deluded by the universal belief in marriage as the panacea of human ills. And yet I did not believe it. I simply shut my eyes to the truths I knew about it, and hoped that my marriage would be an exception.

The race of splendid "bachelor girls" was not born then, or I should have been among them. The unmarried women of my acquaintance were a helpless and a forlorn set, and were often looked upon with contempt. They did not in the least resemble the brilliant, cultured and charming girls who now avoid marriage because they prefer lives of independence, with opportunities of self-culture, to the fate of the generality of their married acquaintances.

Marriage as it has existed in the past, and to-day too for the greater part of humanity, is but a stepping stone to the real, the true, the divine marriage. It is a step in evolution. It is that which perpetuates the race until it shall come into a knowledge of the higher marriage. When this is accomplished, marriage will indeed bring happiness.

In speaking of the drudgery of wives I am not making a reflection on husbands. Marriage is slavery to both husband and wife all the world over, with only here and there an exception. And I am not intimating that true happiness can be found out of marriage under existing conditions; but rather that there is no real happiness on the animal plane of life; and say what you will, we are still living on the animal plane. We have not ascended above it yet, though some of us are beginning to know that there is a higher plane, and we are striking out for it with all the energy we can command.

The race is being prepared through its bitter experiences for the higher marriage that will not prove a disappointment. Even now—almost without knowing the meaning of what it does—it is using every device to escape the entanglements and the drudgery of parenthood.

I hear a thousand voices exclaiming, "Oh! but I love children." Of course you do; the love of the child is but a projection of self-love. Your child is the latest and most vital part of yourself; how can you help loving it?

Again I hear you say, "But the mother love is a divine thing." To which I reply that self-love is a divine thing too; and that it is the redemptive power in the human being. Self-love is the germinal point in the man; it is the centralizing factor about which all that is related to him through his desires comes to him. But to express this self-love in the being of another creature is so much waste of the parents; it is diffusiveness; it is the opposite of concentration; it is the beginning of that self-loss which leads to disease and ends in death.

In saying this I am not trying to make the impression that in the higher marriage there will be no sex interchange. There will still be sex interchange; but under the control of the intellect it will not result in creation on the animal plane. Man in his growth becomes more and more, and not less in any particular. He looses no use that he has acquired in his process of evolution; and those uses are the highest which contribute most to the expression of his happiness. The sex relation will never be disused, but it is even now in process of evolving to a higher use than the mere begetting of children—namely—the quickening into active life of a world of vital intelligence, so high and fine and potent that we may not now even guess its power.

It was my fate to go through the ordinary animal marriage. It was a dreadful experience, but I needed it, and I do not regret it. If I had not passed through it I should have missed the foundation for the most valuable knowledge I have acquired. But of this marriage I will not speak yet.

As I approached womanhood my girl friends were often talking to me about their lovers. It seemed as though they were always in love with some one, or some one was always in love with them. The matter perplexed me. I really did not know what it meant; but it did seem a most desirable condition to be in. · I thought of it a good deal as I had thought of the chills and fever, and longed for an attack of it.

I had two offers of marriage before I was fourteen, which I did not think worth considering. The first one came when I was scarcely more than twelve. Here now I have a granddaughter just twelve years old who seems like a baby to me; but I did not seem at all like a baby to myself at that age; and indeed I had achieved my full height, and weighed precisely one hundred and fifty-one pounds. I was weighed on my twelfth birthday in the same room and at the same time with a little, old, "pussy" farmer from the country named Ham Crumbley. He was all stomach with spindle legs and a bald head. We weighed in the same notch exactly, which gave me the impression that I looked like him, or was intangibly connected with him in a manner dreadful to think about. No previous event of my experience humiliated me so much since aunt Clem found the resemblance between old Johnny Young and me at the fitting of my first pair of drawers.

Jim Whitney was not of "our set," though probably he did not know it. It is altogether more probable he thought there could be no set so exclusive as not to include him; but we knew it; we were quite sure he did not belong to the Fairfield "four hundred." Jim—besides having a tow head, that we made fun of unmercifully—had the "big head" also. His opinion of himself was the most colossal psychological structure ever built on so frail a foundation. It was amusing, when it was not aggravating, to hear him tell of the number of girls in love with him, and gravely ask advice as to which one he had better marry. He was the "orneriest" looking man in town, so aunt Sally Linthecum said, and I think she might have said the state, and still have been within bounds. She did not see how he could live in the same house with himself, and not just give right up and die of disgust. And yet he "actilly, *actilly*" thought himself a "poragon," he was that "pompeyed" in his own opinion.

Jim dressed better than most of our town boys; but he was little and insignificant looking, with a face that resembled the blossom end of a cocoanut more than anything else. I never dreamed of being the favored one of his affections until one Sunday he called at our house arrayed more gorgeously than I had ever seen him. Mother was present, but after a few minutes she excused herself and left us alone. She had not got fairly out of the room when all in a second I knew Jim's business; and I knew that mother knew; and I knew perfectly well that she was on the other side of the parlor door listening and choking her laugh down. All this I knew without knowing; and I actually believe I broke out all over with prickly heat, so fearful was the rush of blood to the surface of my body, and so instantaneous was the panic that seized me. It was another case of Sister Martha. I had not in the least regained possession of myself when I saw him on his knees before me repeating something he had either composed beforehand or committed to memory out of a dime novel. I can only recall—"Oh, thou most seraphic, angelic being! Thou art the sun of my existence towards which my soul turns as the needle to the pole. Thou most beautiful—" * * *

At this juncture he stopped suddenly, and not without good cause. If this little twelve-year-old grandchild of mine should do what I did then it would not surprise me at all; but to think that I did it seems actually an improbable thing. What I did was to jump into his tow hair with both hands and make it fly like pollen from a dandelion seed pod. I snatched it out with such vicious rapidity that he could scarcely scramble to his feet. But he did get up after a few seconds and rush into the street bareheaded; then he rushed back and seized his hat, and out he dashed again looking as wild as a hawk. I do not think he heard what I had been listening to for some seconds—the illy repressed breathings indicating that mother was almost in a hysterical state from her effort to keep from laughing out loud.

This offer of marriage did not put me on a level with the other girls in any way. I could not boast of it as they boasted of their offers, and so I said nothing about it; and I told mother flat-footed that if she ever mentioned it to any one I would drown myself. I do not believe she ever told it, though I am sure it must have nearly killed her to keep from it.

I was fourteen years old when my second offer came. This second offer afforded me no more gratification than the first one did so far as giving me a chance to boast of it to the other girls. The gentleman from whom I received it did not belong to "our set" either.

I had been in Salem on a visit to some friends there, and was starting home again. The morning was as pleasant as could be. It was in the spring and everything was coming into leaf, and the air was mild and delicious. Salem is forty miles from Fairfield. Just now it is coming in for a large share of notice from the newspapers as being the former residence of Mr. Bryan, the Democratic candidate for President. It was a town of not more than five hundred people then, among whom were the Marshalls, Mr. Bryan's near relatives.

There were no railroads, and it was a full day's travel from Salem to Fairfield. As the stage swung around in front of Col. Hainey's residence, where I was staying, it was packed full, three on a seat. The driver asked if I was willing to ride outside with him. So I clambered up and made myself comfortable on the highest perch to be had, and away we went with four splendid, great, gray horses in front.

I have tried every species of locomotion from a bicycle to an elephant, and it is my belief that there is nothing equal to a stage ride. To be sure our stage riding in southern Illinois was rather monotonous over flat prairies and wooded bottom lands, with here and there a plunge through some lovely stream; but I have had experiences in stage riding the memory of which will go with me a long, long time yet. It was in the mountain regions of California where I wrung from this experience the bewilderingly exalted emotions that add depth and breadth to the ordinary scope of life. Oh! the dauntless joy of the thing; the grip-on-fate feeling; the fearlessness—not recklessness—far from it, but absolute fearlessness, engendered by a sense of mastery for which there is no precedent, but which seems to rest on a foundation surer than any precedent can give. There is something truly divine in this feeling. With me it was a realization of my own deathlessness; it was nothing short of the temporary externalization of spirit or will; that part of me which is absolute; that breath of the infinite which cannot die. It came through my body and proclaimed itself invincible.

How many times I have taken the stage at Lower Lake, near which place I was living, for the purpose of reaching Calistoga, some thirty miles away. The soft, magnetic air of that peculiar climate transfused my whole being; the beautiful horses were themselves an inspiration. Trotting or walking every movement seemed to be gauged by the finest steel springs, as we travelled along toward the base of Mt. Saint Helena. Here we crossed a stream that often was only a thread of silver, and again a raging torrent; then the slow, laborious crawl up the mountain side until we reached the toll house on top. I will not describe the scenes that spread out before us, changing constantly as we ascended. They were not particularly wild, but very varied, and to me lovely. There is grander scenery in California than this, but this never tired me, no matter how frequently I passed over the road. Each grade of beauty in nature finds its response in one of the numberless phases of the human mind.

At the toll house fresh horses would be waiting for us, one man to a horse. The driver got down from his perch and examined the wagon; examined the harness on the four fresh horses. One could not help observing the fine sense of mastery expressed in his face. His conquests had been in the animal realm, but they were undoubted conquests; no man ever wore that look but there was a reason for it. Swinging back to his place the wide awake observer would notice the contraction of the muscles in his fine arm, and the splendid breast, whose broad, deep development in 'a man always gives one a conviction of tenderness as well as strength.

"Turn 'em loose, boys. Now then!" And the horses were in the air that very instant on a mad run, and never would they break step until we reached the plain some miles below. Sometimes the coach was on three wheels as we zigzagged round one of the sudden bends; sometimes it was on two wheels; now and then it was on one wheel, and once in a long time there were no wheels touching ground as it scooted around a turn above some fearful incline. There were broken bones and a few deaths on that road, but not many; and when accidents happened, the driver was strange to the business, and wore no such face as the one I have described.

Poor, splendid Hank Monk was the prince of stage drivers. For twenty years he drove every day over the Sierra Nevada Range. But one day he was sick; he could not go. Presently he became delirious and in his burning fever he was on the stage box again talking to his old friends, the horses. "Steady now, boys; you know this slide as well as I do; go slow. What's the matter with the light? Its gettin' dark long before it ought to! Steady, boys; steady!" He was now making strong movements with his right foot. Then he rested as if in despair, and with a voice so truly tragic it started the hair on the heads of those about him he said, "I'm on the down grade and can't reach the brake." These were his last words, and they were spoken as if the responsibility of lives was resting on him, and he was powerless to help.

The responsibility of lives had been resting on him for many years, and he had not ceased to feel it and to be true to it. Where is the monument for these staunch souls who have never flinched in the face of duty? Where but just where it ought to be, close locked in the hearts of a thousand nameless ones who owe so much to them for the splendid patterns of humanity they have furnished.

But see how I have wandered from that early stage ride, when as a child woman I sat perched on the box with the driver, perfectly enraptured with the sense of beauty forced on me by the flowers and trees and running brooks and the banks of pearly clouds. I never saw the time when I have not felt the loveliness of this lovely world.

The driver sometimes spoke to me, and I answered him civilly, but coldly. He was not of "our set"; he must not presume. Still, with my wide-awake perception of beauty I could not help observing the fine athletic grace of his form and movements as he let himself down or climbed back to the box, which he did quite frequently in fixing the harness, watering the horses, etc. After a time I noticed him more carefully. He was young; his face was clean shaven; his features were of a grand type; his expression indicated character; his dress—though of cheap stuff, was perfectly clean, and could not at all conceal the magnificent proportions of his splendid form. The word handsome does not describe him, and even at that early age I knew it. I had no respect then any more than now for what was considered the ordinary masculine beauty; and it was with a judgment ahead of my years that I measured him. I felt his superiority, though I could not have described it.

I saw also that he wished to please me, and that his eyes lit up beautifully if ever for a moment my eyes met them. But it was seldom that this happened, and when it did happen it was simply to rebuke the feeling that was growing in him for me.

The idea of a stage driver daring to fall in love with me. He did not know the aristocratic stock from which I was descended. I wondered what grandfather Ridgeway would say if he knew about it.

I had been educated in a way to make me feel the sacredness of caste quite as much as any Brahmin; and the Ridgeways were an exclusive race. So at least their boasting had made them appear in my sight. Mother had sometimes gone East to visit the relatives there; and she talked a good deal of the splendors of the wealthy Ridgeways of Philadelphia. Old John Jacob Ridgeway who was the confessed rival financially of John Jacob Astor; and uncle Tom Ridgeway who was very rich and lived in grand style.

And the tribe of Wilmans was not an inch behind. Indeed there were tales of almost royal descent connected with the Wilmanses. Grandfather Wilmans was a German; and Germany was so far away in those days that it was easy to credit the old gentleman with having been a baron at least. This belief was very strong among the people, though I never heard it talked of by my grandfather at all. Indeed grandfather Wilmans was a strangely reticent man, and never said anything to throw light on the reports about him. But it is a fact that he did no work, had no business of any kind, and drew a large sum annually from Germany and lived in great style for that time and place.

So we had quite a large supply of family pride to

live up to; and it is no wonder that I should have looked upon this young man very much as I would have looked on an unusually fine horse. And this is just what I did. And yet there was something so manifestly distinguished in his face that I hesitated more than once before I settled it as a fact that he was a stage driver and nothing more.

He was quite illiterate as his language demonstrated; and it was perfectly clear that he was no equal of mine, and had no right to think he was. But what an astonishingly bright face he had, and how gentle his manner was towards me. Each mile of our journey added to his interest in me until—except for his unfortunate grammer—he might have been a prince paying the most delicate attentions to the princess of his choice.

About a week after I reached home the mail brought me a letter from him, and it contained an offer of marriage. It was written in a school-boy hand, and I do not believe there was a capital letter in it from beginning to end.

The letter was absolutely useless. I could not show it to my girl friends at all. I carried it in the bosom of my dress for a week with the secret pride that I had had a real, sure-enough offer, and yet with the chagrin that it came from a stage driver and was ungrammatical in its construction.

My thoughts for the author of the letter were about as considerate as those of a Newfoundland puppy for the rag doll it is tearing up. Indeed I did not think of him at all, and never answered his letter, and never saw him again—at least, not for many years.

I did see him again, and under very changed circumstances. I was married and living in California, an overworked farmer's wife with four children. I had scarcely been off the farm for years except to the nearest village. Something prompted me to go to the State fair at Sacramento. My husband, Dr. Baker, fought the proposition as usual, but I would not yield, and went, taking every chick and child along. The opening speech was made by the governor of the state. I had taken too little interest in politics to know or care anything about the late gubernatorial election beyond the fact that the name of one of the rival candidates was familiar to me, but as it was a very common name I thought nothing of it.

When the speaker arose he was greeted with great applause. I turned cold all over, though the day was blazing hot; for right before me, and not very far away, was the identical stage driver who had offered himself to me. He was handsomer than ever: not with commonplace good looks, but with the look of matured mastery, coupled with the original beauty that had been his rich endowment from nature. There he stood, a fit model for a god, receiving the hearty plaudits of the people who loved him, and not without cause. And there I sat, a worn and faded woman who had passed through enough hardships to kill a herd of Mexican mustangs, and who carried the trace of her overworked and outraged life in every line of a prematurely faded face and form.

CHAPTER XI.

A MOST WORSHIPFUL HERO.

Of course, my readers have noticed that this is not a connected autobiography. It was not my intention to make it such. I only wished to dip into the sunshiny spots of my life, where the green grass was growing, and give little incidents that marked stages of my progress.

But there came a long interval where there was no sunshine; and though I do not like to write of that time, I fear that after a few pages more I shall be forced to do so. But even then, along with the gloom, I managed to extract a little coloring that went a good way toward relieving it.

I was a happy disposition; or perhaps it would be more true to say that I had the most inexhaustible vitality I have ever seen in any living soul; man or woman. It actually seemed as if nothing could crush me.

Like a child, when hurt to the quick I kept hunting something to amuse me and take my thoughts away from the smart. I think this disposition was the thing that helped me to bear the bluffs and insults I received in childhood with so much indifference. They would have hurt, only I could not bear to think of them, and gradually schooled myself to indifference. I observe that this is characteristic of nearly all children so long as they remain children. The oddity was that I carried the same thing through all my earlier womanhood, and would be carrying it still but for the fact that it has merged into something better; namely, the knowledge that the opinions of most people, and even their actions, are not based on any reasoning of their own, but are exercised as the result of heredity; this condition making them as irresponsible as so many automatons worked by wires whose fastenings are way back in the unthinking past. This being the case I have really no respect for their opinions, and do not care in the least what such persons say of me or think of me, any more than I care for the opinions of the animals—if they have opinions.'

A correct judgment of others will establish the independent thinker in a very free position. It is because we endow others with a judgment superior to our own that their adverse opinions hurt us.

Of course there are persons whose opinions are entitled to our respect, but the number is very small yet. The average man does not think. He hitches his thinking machinery to the thinking machinery of some other person, whose thinking machinery is hitched to another person's still, or to some book which has the authority of numbers to sustain it, if not of brains. And so the masses cling together from the very vacuity of thought; and together they fall upon the person who dares do his own thinking, and in their blind fury they destroy him if they can.

This is not an overdrawn picture of public opinion. It is the most ignorant, irrational thing I know of. Look at it from all sides and judge it—not by the number of people it represents—but by its true character, and then see if you, who are beginning to do your own thinking, can afford to be influenced by it.

The most perfect freedom of all is that which one gains by a true conception of public opinion. To understand its worthlessness liberates us to a wonderful extent; gives us a chance to be our own real selves; enables the "I" within us to stand erect; a thing that very few "I's" have done in this world.

Indeed, I believe I may say that as yet not one has quite done so, though a few have approached a perpendicular attitude. When an "I" shall stand entirely erect, then for the first time the earth will behold a god.

In 1849 the gold fever broke out in California; or rather the fever which had its rise in California broke out all over the United States. Our town and county were shaken up to an extent never known before. Companies organized and made much preparation for "crossing the plains." My father went; and this was the last I ever saw of him, for he died there after five or six years. Instead of bettering his fortune he was ruined financially by the adventure. His mercantile business, which had made him quite a rich man for that part of the country, had been going down for several years before he left. Setting his younger brothers up in business, and paying for their mistakes; doing the same for my mother's brothers, and going security for everybody who asked him, finally brought him face to face with a very perplexing situation. He thought to mend matters by going to the Golden State and picking up a fresh fortune. He went, but did not get the fortune, and so put off his return from year to year until death overtook him suddenly.

About six months before the California fever broke

out, a gentleman took up his abode in Fairfield, with whom all the ladies in town were mightily pleased. When I saw him first he was walking from the hotel to our store. His appearance was something of an excitement even to my phlegmatic nature. He was of a splendid height, and magnificently formed; a veritable Hercules in strength, and an Adonis in beauty. Perhaps what struck me more than his noble proportions was his fine clothes; real, sure-enough "store clothes," and no mistake, all topped off with a silk hat.

"Store clothes" is not a high-sounding phrase now, but the very reverse. At that time, however, the phrase had reference more to the material than to the make. It was before the day of ready-made clothing. It pointed the fact that his clothes were not of the homespun cloth that our farmers' wives manufactured into garments for their husbands and sons, but were made of fine, glossy, imported and expensive goods.

There was not a particle of the fop or pretender about him. I knew that at a glance. He certainly did look to be a very manly man. He interested me from the first moment I saw him. It was not the interest that men usually awaken in women; it was rather that I looked upon him as a curiosity. I kept thinking of him and wanted to see him at closer range, just as a child who catches a glimpse of the elephant as it disappears through the doors of the circus tent wants to get a better view of it.

It was not many days before I was gratified. He came to our house and begged mother as a great favor to board him. He could not stand the hotel; and no wonder for it was beyond toleration by anyone but some transient customer who had to stop there or in the street.

I had no idea that mother would receive him in the family, as she had never taken a boarder before; but she did, and gave him the best room in the house. I discovered afterwards that every one of my aunts, as well as mother, had made up their brilliant minds that the Lord had sent this gorgeous individual for the special purpose of marrying me. He was a doctor and had come to locate. I think he was the only doctor in town who was regularly equipped with that essential of the craft called a diploma. He had graduated at old Ben Dudley's Institution in Lexington, Kentucky. He was not a very young man, being as much as thirty-five years old, and he was engaged to be married to the daughter of the Governor of the state. This sounded big; and I expect it put a check on the dawning hopes of my uncles and aunts and cousins; but somehow it did not dampen my irrepressible spirits.

I had been taught to look up to men as superior creatures, and it was years and years before I discovered my mistake; and yet the critical spirit was wide awake in me, with a strong inclination to trust my own opinion of them, and to measure them with the same judgment that I measured women. But the force of education was too strong, and I was almost compelled by the family idolatry of this person to feel myself complimented by his attentions. Not that his attentions meant anything more at that time than a little polite appreciation of my social and literary merits, of which my friends were very proud. He told us, and told everybody of his engagement, and evidently considered it a great feather in his cap.

I am held for a moment by the words "social and literary," that I have just used about myself. I actually wrote poetry in those days, and it was gladly accepted by our one little botched and dreadfully printed weekly paper. It was very difficult for any one to make good sense of the stuff after it was published; partly because the print was so imperfect, but principally because there was no sense in it. But it was called poetry, and nobody seemed to know the difference; and I was wreathed in glory. If an original poem was to be read on the fourth of July who but I should write it? If a baby died it was a consolation to the parents to have a poem written about it. Mercy! how much work it was to write one; what cudgeling of brains; what adroit pilfering from other poets; no not *other* poets, but poets; how hard it was to work in such expressions as "the Lord giveth, the Lord hath taken away; blessed be the name of the Lord!" In the first place the words were as hard to lead into any correct measure as a lot of untrained pigs to market; and in the second place I could not forebear some original cogitations about the Lord's right to take away what he had once given. It involved a question of morality to me that threatened to wreck my theology. But always in some way— by sheer force of animal will, I expect—I got over the difficulties and produced what was required of me, and it satisfied my appreciative audience.

Now, Dr. Baker—for this was my new friend's name—was no better judge of my articles than the rest of the community, even though he was fairly educated; and he too thought me a genius and did not withhold his praise.

Matters stood in this state of gentle admiration from him towards me for quite a long time; I cannot recall how long. But I did not like him much. I tried to, because my entire family were in a state of perspiring worship for him, and their condition put its compulsion on me to be likewise. But no, he had grown commonplace. The novelty of his superb upholstering wore off so that I lost respect for it; and when the cat had kittens one night in his silk hat I was glad of it, though I concealed my feelings and put on a face of hypocritical regret to keep mother from scolding me. It would have been just like her to suspect that I had taken that immaculate head gear down from its peg and put it where "Crazy Jane" could make use of it; so it behooved me to be sorrowful; and I was.

The same sort of compulsion was on me when at last he professed to love me. I cannot recall just why his engagement with the Governor's daughter was broken off; but I believe she married a rich man and left him out in the cold. I ought to know all about it, for I lived with him a good many years after that, and often heard him repeat the circumstances to the coarse crowds he gathered around him, and swear over the perfidy of women until even the listening "bull whackers," as the cow boys were called then, turned white about the gills. But there is such a thing as hearing a narrative repeated so often you lose the sense of it, and cannot repeat it yourself. And as these particular outbursts had their origin in a desire to insult me, I took very small notice of them.

But to go back to the time of his jilting, I must say he did not appear to care then, and fell easily into the way of making love to me; a love that I did not dare repulse for fear of bringing down the wrath of my family on my head. Why, he was a gentleman—the best educated man and the finest appearing one ever seen in Fairfield! Any woman might be proud to get him for a husband. Contrast him with the town boys, and see the difference. And here were my family from the oldest down, except my father, who—metaphorically—were crawling on their stomachs before him in the intensity of their admiration, and no doubt praying the Lord every night to grant them the boon of perpetual relationship through his marriage to me. Even Aunt Sally Linthecum "rastled with God in prar" to this same end. She said so afterwards. And to tell the unvarnished truth it is the only prayer God ever answered for me; and it got me into great trouble; trouble that He never tried to get me out of, though I prayed to Him for years afterwards, until I got disgusted and took the matter in my own hands and easily became liberated. How true it is that God helps those who help themselves; or, in other words, how much easier one can get along without Him than with Him.

I was not really engaged to be married to Dr. Baker when he left with a company overland for California. I received one or two letters from him, which I concealed from mother, and did not answer. Thus the matter terminated as I supposed; but in reality it had hardly begun.

But something else had begun for us; and that was hard times. We were really poor. Father had left many outstanding accounts for mother to collect, and which would have supported the family if she had collected them. But most of them proved worthless. Father kept sending money along as he could make it, but everything went wrong with him, and he could not send much. I can imagine his distress, for I know his generous nature. He had never withheld anything from his family. Indeed, he loved to have us spend money, and not one of us could recall the time when he would not have made every possible sacrifice for us.

It was after the California crowd had departed, and

we began to feel the grip of poverty, that I regretted how indifferent I had been to every opportunity I had had to get an education. I wanted to go to school and prepare myself for a literary career. I had been flattered a good deal, but fortunately I did not have one bit of confidence in the opinions of my friends concerning my writings; I knew they were trash, and I knew that I had not any of that rare element in my composition called genius. At the same time I felt sure I had something worth more than all the genius in the world, and nobody guessed what it was; nor did I define it, though I knew it was within me then as well as I know it now.

How shall I describe it? It was a kind of fortitude, a power to bear and endure and never yield and never be discouraged, that always rested me when I went down within myself. It was not courage, but more than courage; it was not vitality, but more than vitality; it was not hope, but certainty; it was not the promise of more life, but the indestructible principle of life itself. It was the perfect assurance of success in any career I might undertake; it was solid ground and rich in the promise of bearing, no matter what kind of seed I planted in it. It was the self-hood of me, the invincible "I."

The frothy surface me used to go down into the depths of this real me and get courage and consolation from it; for it was the incarnation of strength in repose. Moreover, it was the containant of everything I could desire. It was the food and drink, the "green pastures" and "still waters" of my soul. I was at home in it, and I was at home nowhere else.

So, though I knew my poems were trash, I was not discouraged because I trusted this—more than promise—this spirit of infinite fulfillment within me; and trusting it, no blows hurt me except for the moment. Whatever struck me struck that deathless something that could neither be bruised nor killed.

Now this, in its external manifestation, was a spirit of wonderful endurance. It was even more; it was a kind of fearlessness that overrode temporary disappointments, which—taken in connection with my sense of humor—gave me a happy disposition and made a great laugher of me.

During these years I had to a considerable extent dropped the shadow of brother Findlay's religion. The current of life within was too strong to tolerate it. I had not reasoned myself out of it, but had become too vital for its death-dealing influence to cloud me more than a few hours at a time, on occasions of church revivals, etc.

I was thinking more of getting an education than anything else. One day I got hold of Madame De Stael's "Corinne" and became enthused by it. There was something in the book that operated on my ignorant mind like wine. I felt that all the barriers to my long cherished wish were removed, and that the way would now open; and it did.

There had only been one obstacle all the time, and that was lack of money. Where would the money come from? My brother Ivens was "printer's devil" in Mr. Stickney's office on a salary of two dollars a week, and that never paid. But some undreamed of windfall put it in Mr. Stickney's power to pay him.

The amount was $20. The little fellow brought it to me with his sweet dark eyes all aglow, and told me I could have it to go to school on.

Immediately afterwards a neighbor told me that she had relatives in Jacksonville, Illinois, and was going to visit them, and asked me to go with her in the large family carriage.

Now, Jacksonville was the goal of my ambition. It was a college town; and another thing that seemed to point in the line of my desires was the fact that I knew a splendid family there who were distant relatives, and who liked me very much. Mr. James Dickens was a methodist preacher as poor as a church mouse, with a heart big enough to compensate for the smallness of his purse. I could go there almost without cost, and if things did not shape themselves my way, I could come home when my friends returned.

On my way to Jacksonville I saw my first train of cars. The Illinois Central was the only railroad in the state; and I am under the impression that it had then been in operation but a short time. The family and I got out of the carriage when we came to the crossing, and looking away for miles and miles along the perfectly straight track stretching through the seemingly boundless prairie to the far horizon line, we saw something moving towards us no larger than a man's hat. It was a coming train. I watched it increase in size, as it approached, with feelings of indescribable exultation and a swelling sense of man's power that I had never felt before; and when with a rush and a roar that made us tremble for our safety, it plunged past with all the windows open and passengers waving hats and handkerchiefs at us, I turned insane for the moment—or sane, rather—and found myself saying to God, "What ails you that you let man's work beat your own? It is time you stopped crowing and went to work to do some practical good."

Jogging along in the old carriage the remainder of the afternoon I became deeply repentant over the unprecedented burst of reason that had flooded my theology for the moment, and prayed for forgiveness as I had very seldom prayed before.

CHAPTER XII.

SCHOOL AGAIN.

Occasionally I pick up a paper and begin to read some sap-headed story of college days. I drop it like a hot potato, and rush off to one of the books of some old scientist to get the taste out of my mouth. The insipidity, the almost nauseating egotism of these exceedingly young persons as told in the novels printed about them, and their verdant proceedings, is beyond the power of matter-of-fact people to endure.

Yet here I am doing the same thing. I would not have believed it of myself.

After all there must be some fault in the way these stories are told; some lack of nature in their unfoldment. They do not truly represent the young people. They "endanger the lives of their clients by trying to stretch them up into giants." We feel the spirit of exaggeration that conceals and mars the real beauty which surely does abound there. The college boys themselves, outside of these stories, are full of interest to me. It seems as if I can never get done laughing at them and with them; not in the way of ridicule, let me tell you, but out of pure sympathy in their irrepressible spirits, their nonsense and fun. I love them dearly; and when a crowd of them boards a street car in which I sit placidly, the whole atmosphere changes; the sparkle of champagne comes in it; I get young immediately, carrying back to this renewed youth a deeper understanding of the boys than they themselves have; for I see them glorified by the knowledge their latent capacities hold in abeyance.

The thing I like best about the boys is their naturalness. Girls become distorted by being made to try to appear pretty and sweet. Too many of them are always conscious of the public eye. But not so with the boys. Through the bur of their unconsciousness you see their native goodness and sweetness; and it is a strange woman who does not feel like adopting almost every one she sees.

When I reached Jacksonville I found my friend, Mr. Dickens, who immediately shouldered my responsibilities and bridged the way for my entering the Methodist Episcopal Conference Female College. I suppose it would be offended if I were to abridge its title. Mr. Jaques was president; and he consented to let me enter the school without paying the annual fee in advance. I was expected to go into the country and teach during the three months vacation that came every year, and out of my earnings I was to pay this bill. Mr. Dickens and his good wife would board me and trust the Lord for their pay, which was only two dollars a week. I am glad to say that I did not have to call on my security, but paid them constantly and lovingly by sharing everything I had with them; last of all an unexpected piece of good luck that happened to me, of which I shall presently speak.

If I am not mistaken Mr. Dickens' salary was only four hundred dollars a year. He had a small farm in the country near Jacksonville that was rented out to his eldest son, Washington, who only came home occassionally on a visit. The second child was Kate, a girl near my own age. After Kate came Benny and Jim and Shug. Shug was the youngest. I do not recall her true name or know whether she had one. Shug was used as a contraction of sugar and applied to her because of her sweetness.

Jacksonville, Illinois, was then the college town of the state. It was a beautiful place of ten thousand people; peculiar people too. I wonder if the inhabitants of all college towns are not in a measure dominated by the superabundant vitality of the students, who swarm the thoroughfares and places of resort, lead in the amusements and constitute an ever ubiquitous element like the air that people must breathe, until they become of the same nature that it is.

To me Jacksonville was a city. I had never seen so large a town before. The stores were splendid—so I thought then—and how Kate and I longed for some of the goods on display in the windows. Sometimes we went in and made our small purchases and walked away regretfully. If I had been a princess royal I could not have been treated more courteously. The manners of the salesmen were very marked, and I was always urged to purchase more. At several places we were coaxed to run bills; but for a long time we declined to do so. I was well dressed when I left home, and for nearly a year I made my garments serve me. I had passed one vacation, during which time I earned enough by teaching school in the country to pay for past tuition, books, etc., at the college, and a little for Mr. Dickens; but not a dollar did I have for myself.

Kate would have gone in debt to the merchants if her parents had not prevented it. But at last I was forced to do so. Later I became well acquainted with a nice young clerk who told me about the system. He said the merchants were safe in giving the girls goods on credit, and rarely lost a dollar. In a great percentage of cases the parents paid the bills; in a few cases the girls married, and the husbands, under a law then in force, had to pay debts contracted by the wife before marriage. It was well understood that in any case a debt lay heavily on the mind of a girl or woman, and she never rested until it was paid. This was a peculiarity the merchants were always ready to take chances on.

For my part I knew how heavily it rested on one girl's mind, but that did not restrain me. I began to dress beautifully, though not extravagantly; and I made my own dresses, having excellent talent in that direction. But the better I dresssed the more shabbily did Kate and her dear mother appear. So I bought clothes for them and the children, and we were all very happy, and unhappy also, in consequence. If I could only have known how it would terminate my heart would have been sufficiently lightened to have enjoyed the situation better.

In the meantime I was making a record in the college. I was exercising—without knowing its power—the great secret of the age, of all ages—which is that persistent effort conquers, no matter what the opposition may be. Nay, more; that it *creates* out of nothing, as it were, anything on which the desire is centered.

I had not been three months in college before I felt myself a leader in every branch of study; and a social leader also. I was a leader by virtue of the reason that I did not care to lead. My head was full of an ideal to be achieved. And though this ideal was so indistinct that I could not have defined it, yet it was always before me like some veiled thing of such dazzling beauty I scarcely dared ask to behold it uncovered, and was satisfied to leave it in the varying cloud tints of its ever changing loveliness. This imaginative thing became the polar star of my destiny, and took many a fanciful shape before I knew what it meant and what it was.

At the present time, though years and years have passed, I only know in part; but it is still my ever faithful guide that I never tire in following, even when it leads me so far from the beaten track of thought that I am momentarily overcome and lost in a sense of indescribable loneliness.

If I had been left alone then to simply grow in the

direction of my ideal, I scarcely dare imagine what would have been the result. It would have been heaven on earth. Of this I am sure; for heaven exists here, and men are bound to come into a consciousness of it sooner or later. I had it within my grasp, but lost it for the time by plunging into the pessimistic spirit of the age and taking up the cudgel in defence of the wrongs of others. I had not learned that people's wrongs are their rights; so long as they have not overcome them by intelligent thought and action; and so I descended into the chaos that was tearing a nation in two, and did all I could to make "confusion worse confused."

It was the well-meant mistake of my friend, Mr. Dickens. Slavery was the crying sin of the age. It must be wiped out. It was the religious duty of every person to use all his power to crush the monster of iniquity. All of which was right enough. It was only the methods we used that were wrong. Hammer and tongs—fire and sword, instead of the culture that unfolds man out of the beast.

"You, Helen," he would say, "are a glorious writer;" (he really thought so, I am sure; though I knew quite well that he was not capable of judging the literary merits of any writings.) "You are a glorious writer.

God has committed rare gifts to your keeping and you must expend them in his service; you must make all of your writings run in the direction of the emancipation of slavery." And then he would unload his own ideas upon me until my vivid, red-headed temperament caught fire and I would write pages and pages of stuff that was tense and turgid with the wrongs of a race, and with the wrath that ought to be awakened in its defense. Mr. Dickens said that such wrath was divine; and I was too young to know that every form of wrath is a mistake, and can never take the place of the calm, cool *reason* that has a right to control all things, and whose mission it is to guide without any help from either the passions or emotions.

My articles were sought by the editor of the one anti-slavery paper of the place to whom Mr. Dickens showed them. It was a bold man that dared publish a word in defense of the slave; but this was not in the earliest days of agitation on the subject, or he would have been mobbed, as several others were. The public had—at the time of which I am writing—been swayed to a considerable extent by the still earlier pioneer in this crusade, and the people were beginning to think deeply, and in a spirit of justice. Nevertheless the idea was not popular, and was not respectable.

This was several years before the war. It was the spirit of the war brewing for the outbreak that every one dreaded, and that eventually came.

President Jaques wisely prohibited me from reading these compositions in the school, as even the publication of my ideas in the paper was already causing him anxiety.

It had been the habit of the school to give public exhibitions monthly, at which times our large hall was filled to overflowing. By a sort of unspoken consent I had been put forward at these exhibitions in a way to make me a favorite with the people. When at last it dawned on the Faculty that—taking all things into consideration—I was becoming too prominent, they made an effort to keep me in the back ground; an effort the audiences resented by calling for me vociferously and persistently; especially those who knew how I stood on the slavery question. It was evident that the people were taking sides more openly than they had ever done; and the amount of bitter hostility between the factions gathered strength steadily and forcefully. It looked as if I had planted a seed that threatened to disrupt the school. A few Southern patrons had withdrawn their daughters, and others seemed inclined to do so. Nothing could have been worse for the financial success of the institution, and I saw it and regretted that any feeling had been awakened; for I loved President Jaques and never had a better friend. Many a conversation have we had on the subject, all terminating in the belief that neither I nor anyone was to blame; that the curse of an awful wrong was upon us, that was justly pushing us toward a catastrophe which would prove at once our punishment and the slave's restitution. In the meantime I refused to answer the public demand to appear at the monthly entertainments, and the time rolled along to the day of our graduation.

There were twenty of us in the graduating class. Our compositions were limited to a few pages, and were as jejune and insipid as such essays usually are. All would have passed off well but for a mistake of President Jaques.

A speech that was supposed to be a sort of a brief review of the affairs of the college during the past year was a part of the programme. This was delivered by the President. In the speech he referred to the rumor that the school was becoming tinctured with the anti-slavery feeling, and denied that this was true, claiming that no faintest touch of political sentiment had been permitted to enter into it at all. A man—

one of the wealthiest citizens in the place, and one of the haughtiest social leaders—rose impetuously and said boldly that the statement of the President was a mistake; that the anti-slavery sentiment in the school was dominating everything; and the most contemptible part of it was that the Faculty, not daring to shoulder the responsibility of its own opinions, had put them forth through the pen of a gifted but misguided girl—a member of the present graduating class—Miss Helen Wilmans.

I must explain that up to the time of which I am writing one could speak in favor of slavery with impunity; it was only against slavery that no word was permitted—so greatly did the Southern spirit dominate every department of our social life. The voices of the thousands whose souls were seething in an almost uncontrollable wrath, that such an institution should be tolerated in a republic that called itself "free," were under the compulsion of silence. They had to hold themselves in check, and see cruelty and injustice piled mountain high and capped with the haughty insolence of a people whose pride had been fed by triumphs in congress and obsequious flattery from Northern compeers, together with the daily incense that constituted the home breath of their lives, arising from the fears incident to the subjugated manhood of a race. Government was backing this side; the anti-slavery position was treasonable. Heavens! what flames of wrath were smouldering under that word "treasonable."

After this accusation made by one of the most influential men in the state, President Jaques' courage must have forsaken him for the time. He entered into an explanation which was surely an unwise thing. But even this he could have made without implicating me; but in his excitement and weakness he blundered into an attempt to exonerate the college at my expense.

He said that from the first he had found it an almost impossible thing either to guide or repress me; that I had been utterly unmanageable. He accused me of ingratitude towards the school, the teachers and himself. And much more to this purpose. I sat behind him with the other girls on the platform and heard it all, *for the first time.* He had never given me a hint of such feeling as he expressed for me. On the contrary he had been my best friend; a friend whose true tenderness and loving pride in me had shown in his eyes and conduct from first to last during the two years of my stay there. I had never entered his presence in a single instance that his kind eyes did not brighten as they caught mine. He was proud of me as a student; tender of me as if I had been his own sister; his appreciative laugh always responded to my nonsense; and never once in those years had I received a word or sign of reproval from him. I trusted and loved him.

After he had finished there was a deep silence, and then commotion and confusion. Several persons were on their feet all speaking at once. For my part I felt bitterly wronged. A complete recognition of the whole situation lit up my intellect, and I seemed to be pure spirit. I stepped to the front of the stage. The wrangling in the audience ceased, and the most complete silence followed. I said, "If there is no other soul in all the world who dares lift voice in defense of an outraged and a cruelly oppressed people, I dare." And then I went on in a tone of voice that seemed perfectly level, only for the slight tremor that showed unmistakably how every word was quivering over latent fire; and the fire burst forth presently. I did not spare the cowardice of the people nor the dastardly character of the situation. I said my say to the uttermost; said it strongly but briefly; and then I asked if I was to be excluded from my share in a collegiate education because I would not compromise with the vilest sin of the age? President Jaques had never expected it of me. He had never rebuked me for my opinions; I denied it here in his presence, and could not reconcile the words he had just spoken with all his past kindness and gentleness to me. Why, he was my dearest friend. I tried to say "I loved him," but a choking sob came in place of the words, and it was answered by other sobs from the audience. Then I gathered strength again and said, "Of all the results of a disguised position the worst I had ever witnessed had been brought about to-day, when a man whose heart was so great and whose life was so pure had stood face to face with a sentiment so debased as to weaken his manhood until he dared not speak the truth."

Then I sat down, with a swimming head, and can scarcely tell what followed. The class song was sung and the diplomas distributed, yet not for one moment was there anything but the tensest excitement among the people. The excitement was pressed down, but it was there; and it made one feel as if he were on the verge of a volcano in momentary expectation of an eruption.

Hastily written notes were being passed up to me

from the audience, but I could not read them; I could only receive them and let them fall, owing to the nerveless condition of my hands. A girl near me took them and gave them to me later. They contained bank bills for various sums; and one was a fifty-dollar "slug" of California mintage, the first coin of its kind I ever saw.

The thing came to an end at last, and I found myself in the midst of a crowd where hundreds of people were trying to shake hands with me. But I recall that others stood apart and looked at me malignantly. Last of all, and that which left the most indelible impression, was the face of President Jaques. I looked upon it with eyes out of which the light of all happiness had departed, to find the same deadness in his. He looked as if he had turned to stone. I made my way to the door where Mr. Dickens had a carriage waiting. I never saw my beloved teacher again.

Oh! the happy hours I had spent with him; oh! the rejoicing I had had in his pride in me. Always he would come into the class room like a prince, his face calm to coldness; glancing round with eyes of swift intelligence, simply sweeping the group, his look would be arrested when it met mine, and then his face would become illuminated. Even yet I think of him tenderly, though his beautiful form has been under the sod for years and years.

I recall one instance when his hopes of my future had received reinforcement from an unexpected quarter.

The occasion was this. The graduating class was assembled in order to recite a lesson in "Mental Science." This was the name of the text book. I cannot recall the author, but a shallower treatise on the human mind and its powers was never written. The girls did not pretend to study it, and, indeed, the most of them were very indifferent students. But I had been quite faithful in the matter, and it usually devolved on me to answer the most of the questions.

"Who knows this lesson?" I asked, as soon as I entered the room.

"You, if anybody," said some one.

"I have not even looked at it," I replied.

"Then may the Lord have mercy on our souls," said another girl: and we looked at each other and giggled. I had no time to even glance the lesson then, for the door opened and President Jaques came in and another gentleman with him. The questions began and none of us knew anything. Mr. Jaques was embarrassed. At length he said to me, "Miss Wilmans, it is unusual for you to put your teacher to shame by such utter neglect as this."

I said, "I did not think of putting you to shame, Mr. Jaques. My only thought was that I had had enough of this book, and did not care to waste more time on it."

Then the strange gentleman said, "So you do not approve of the book; what is the matter with it?"

As I looked at him he smiled, and there was my mother's smile exactly. Then I saw that his features were like hers, and that in every particular he might have been her twin brother, the resemblance between them was so striking. My heart warmed towards him instantly, and I did not feel the least hesitation in talking to him. I told him there was not a particle of sense in the book from beginning to end; that the author had invented a theory and had distorted facts to fit it. He asked many questions, and I answered them in a way that seemed to please him. His kind eyes took on a look of the most genial interest. He got out a small note book and put down two or three things I said.

The hour ended and the class was dismissed. As we were passing out Mr. Jaques made a gesture for me to stop. I did so, standing close to the quiet—almost plain looking man whose accidental resemblance to my mother awakened so much love in me. When the door closed I was formally introduced. The name dazed me. Even then it was wreathed with glory. I think I turned pale when I put out my hand and felt it clasped in that of Ralph Waldo Emerson.

But he was saying something earnestly and kindly. I would not have missed hearing it for much. He was asking for my full name. "I want it," he said, "because the world will ring with it some day."

And it was this endorsement of me that President Jaques valued so greatly.

CHAPTER XIII.

A BOY LOVER.

When I saw for the last time the stony, impassive face of my beloved teacher, I was passing out of the college hall forever. There was a carriage waiting, and with Kate and Mr. Dickens I was driven away.

The commotion occasioned by the graduation exercises was great. The town was all excitement. I got both praised and abused, and it was kept up so long that for weeks I was afraid to look through any newspaper for fear of stumbling on my own name. For the circumstances spread, and the press reported them and took sides.

Night after night I was serenaded; and there were songs and music composed to fit the occasion. Oh! how tired I was of it. I wanted to go straight home, but Mr. Dickens—to whom I was as obedient as a child—would not consent. One good thing for me came of all the commotion. I had quite a little sum of money given me on the day I graduated, and more had been sent me. I began to hunt up my store bills in order to pay them; *but every dollar was paid, and I never knew who did it.*

Some two years previous to my going to Jacksonville, my brother Gus had gone to St. Louis, Mo., to attend a medical school. After completing the course he went to Cedar Rapids, Iowa, and located. The town was then a mere village; the whole state was new; it was almost the far West. Gus was an exceedingly attractive young man. He was handsome, gentlemanly, modest, yet self-centered and courageous. He immediately stepped into a fine practice. In less than a year he had purchased one of the best dwelling houses in the place, and had brought my mother and the younger children to him.

Mother would have been very happy in these days but for my father's absence, which was a constant source of sorrow to her. It was this feeling acting upon other feelings that intensified her religious sentiments, and caused her to become almost fanatical on the subject. When at last I broke away from the influence of Mr. Dickens and the loving care of his wife, and went to my mother in her new home, I was chilled and repelled by the atmosphere that emanated from her. Gus was used to it and indifferent to it.

Lib was impervious to any special influences, not being a thinker at all, and having taken mother's advice and joined the church, after which she sank into the lethargy of considering herself all right.

Emma was just about grown, and she certainly was very beautiful and lovely; and the other little girls, Julia and Clem, were sweet children. But it was the deadest household I ever saw. I began to wonder how I should live there long. I resolved that I would not do so, and began to hunt for a situation where I could teach. I at length had an offer from an academy at Griggsville, Ill. This place was not far from Jacksonville. I accepted it and agreed to be there at the opening of the next term, some two months away.

The deadness of our household atmosphere was something so palpable I cannot see how any person could fail to notice it. Gus was changed. Lloyd and Ivens had learned the printer's trade before this, and had situations far from home, so that I did not see them at all on this visit.

What change had taken place in me I do not know; for I am sure that I had changed quite as much as any of the other members of the family. I was no longer one of them. They did not seem to know me, and had no particular interest in me. Emma was kept in the kitchen the most of the time, and I pitied her. The two little ones were found of evenings out on the doorsteps silently watching the stars, their little souls in a strange maze of ignorance. I discovered that they had not the faintest idea of astronomy, and so I began to sit there with them and teach them what I knew. But do what I would the cloud I have spoken of never lifted. Mother held family prayers morning and evening, and practiced all the religious exercises in vogue; and I was used to it and thought it all right, and would not have been satisfied without it; but there was an undercurrent of something somewhere that seemed to be insidiously stealing my vitality, until I became so weak I could scarcely climb the stairs in doing the housework.

What other influences may have aided in producing my condition I cannot tell; but it was one of the great cholera years. In the cities people were dying fast, and a widespread epidemic of fear was in the country.

One morning early I dressed and went down to the basement kitchen to help Emma, who seemed to be chief household servant. There was a bed room opening off the common sitting room, and it was here my mother slept. The door was open and I looked in. The room was in the greatest disorder. Mother tried to speak to me, but could not do so except with her eyes, from which her whole soul looked. I have never seen so much expression in any other eyes, no, never in all my life.

She had been stricken down with cholera so suddenly that it had been impossible for her to let us, who slept on the floor above, know her condition. Emma had passed the open door of the room only a few minutes before, but had not thought to look in. I aroused the household and in a short time every doctor in town was there. It was too late. She lingered a few hours and died.

The one thing that haunted me for years concerning her death was the look with which she followed me wherever I went. If I passed beyond her range of vision her eyes were strained in my direction until I came again within it. What did she want to say? I thought she wished me to promise that I would not desert the children. I put my arms around little Clem and looked at her. A light broke over her face; I was never to desert that child; and I never did.

She had no sooner found that I understood her than her eyes wandered to the other faces. Gus asked her if she was willing to go, and she nodded and smiled yes; and in another moment she was gone. Fourteen other persons lay dead of cholera in the town that same day.

My mother's death was an awful shock. She lay there with her dimpled white hands and her youthful face—for she was little more than a child when I was born—and at her death was less than forty years old, plump and strong and fair, with a face as unbroken as a girl's; and I could not bear it. It seemed as if I could never breathe again. I fell like one smitten with paralysis; and though I did not lose consciousness I lost all power of motion for a day and night, and was weeks in regaining it perfectly.

My mother's death compelled me to change my plans somewhat. I would not relinquish my intention of teaching, but I could not get my consent to leave Emma in the house that I was leaving, she was so lovely and so willing to submit to any work that might be put upon her. I knew that if I should take her that a servant would be provided to do the work, for Lib had never been strong enough to do it. At the same time I was not afraid to leave the two little girls, who had now entered school and seemed much happier than before.

So I took my pretty sister and started on a long journey—made longer by being performed partly by stage, though principally by steamer; and we soon found ourselves back under the roof of my good friend, Mr. Dickens. We were only here a few days, when we went to Griggsville, where my school was ready to open.

Mr. Dickens' family were as loving and hilarious as ever, and I was immediately inducted into the atmosphere of nonsense that pervaded the group in spite of the ever present attempt to keep things down to the level of proper religious solemnity. Really religion was a farce in this family; there was too much human nature about them for this false thing to cover it up; they were too big for so flimsy a cloak, and too intrinsically good to be concealed by it. It was their native goodness which they mistook for religion.

The next morning after we got there we had family prayers as usual. The morning had been chilly and a few sticks were burning in the old-fashioned fire place. The cat I had known so well in the previous years was occupying the choicest corner, big and fat and trifling, but a veritable aristocrat in spite of the fact that he looked as if he had been through a threshing machine, as a result of his dissipated life and his many combats. His ears had entirely departed; one eye was permanently half closed and he seemed to be winking at whomsoever he looked, sardonically and wickedly. The children got out of his way when he manifested an intention of occupying their places, and he would take possession of the vacated seats as if they were his by inalienable right. What was more, he would not stand any nonsense from them. He seemed to know perfectly when they were making fun of him; and as to practical joking he had taught them that such a thing was not to be thought of in connection with his majesty.

A right surly, ugly, defiant old autocrat he was; and more than once during prayers something had happened to roil his temper and put him in a quarrelsome mood.

On this particular morning I think the small boys, Benny and Jim, were anxious to display his peculiarities to Emma, who was unacquainted with them. The little fellows were barefooted even though the morning was chilly. We were all kneeling down, and I was so placed that I could see what the boys were doing. Jim glanced behind him where the cat was lying on the hearth and moved his big toe—very gently at first—but not so gently that the cat failed to see it. He opened one eye a little wider and began to watch. Jim returned to his prayers, but presently moved his toe a trifle more aggressively. The cat— his name was Moses—became alert; he sat up and fastened one villainous eye on Jim's toe. Jim put his head down low on the chair as he continued his devotions. It was not possible to remain in this condition long, in ignorance of what was going on behind him, so he raised his arm and took a look at Moses from under that shelter. Moses knew now that an insult was brewing, for he met Jim's eye with a resolute look, and opened his mouth in a soundless but wicked mew.

Instantly Jim became as one petrified, and remained in this state so long that Moses concluded he had been mistaken in the boy's intentions and was preparing to lie down again, when once more Jim wiggled his toe violently, aggressively, tauntingly. Then Moses split the air with as wicked a yell as I ever heard; not a plain, go-ahead yell, but a complicated, purposeful yell that quavered up and down the gamut, challenging every person in the room to trot out his or her secret intentions towards him and walk up to a settlement. Every hair on his ugly body was on end as he lashed his tail—still continuing his caterwaul with increasing vengeance and an ever changing diversity of tone.

Mr. Dickens suspended his praying and looked around. Every person in the room looked around except Jim, who prayed on with unexampled intentness.

"James," said Mr. Dickens.

"Did you speak to me, pa?"

"Yes, I spoke to you; what have you been doing to Moses?"

Why, pa, I ain't done nothin'; sure as you're born I ain't; I'll cross my heart I haven't touched him."

"James, perhaps you think I am unacquainted with the characteristics of that cat; perhaps you think I am unaware of the fact that it is not necessary to touch him in order to arouse his temper. Whatever may have been the cause of this present outbreak, my son, and I am firmly convinced that you know what it is, I now warn you that it must not occur again during this present season of prayer, which we will now continue."

Moses, who knew perfectly well that his rights were being defended, now lay down, but in a very wide-awake condition, and still growling in undertones. Mr. Dickens prayed away to this accompaniment; and I do not know that I ever heard anything funnier than the mumbled threats of Moses and the variety of tones he managed to express in a rather low, but distinct voice, as the exercises proceeded to a close.

When we arose from our knees and became seated Moses got up also. Evidently he was afraid his temper would cool, and kept coaxing it along on imaginary insults. He watched Jim closely; Jim sat huddled up in a rocking chair with his feet under him. Mrs. Dickens announced breakfast, and we all started toward the dining room. No sooner had Jim's bare feet touched the floor than Moses sprang upon them like a tiger, his fur on end, his claws unsheathed as with frantic movements he tore away at the little fellow's unprotected flesh. Jim's nimbleness saved him from serious damage, but it was hours before Moses was sufficiently quieted to go to sleep on his favorite mat in the chimney corner; and although Jim denied the impeachment, it was a long time before he "winked his toe" at the old savage again.

A few days later Emma and I were in Griggsville at "Pap Wageley's" hotel, where we remained a few days before we found a private boarding house to suit us; after which the school in which I was to teach opened, and I began my duties.

Oh, the stupidity of the situation! I did not want to teach, but it was teach or starve. And I was lonesome; I had been lonesome for such a long time. Emma was the only creature on earth who drew my heart out in affection. I hardly know what this condition meant. One thing certain, the cloud that was over me seemed very heavy and impenetrable. Religion was not troubling me much. I was quite devout and had a feeling of satisfaction in my devotions. My salary was small, but enough to satisfy my wants. I had lost the desire for fine clothes for myself, but loved to see Emma dressed. It was the one spark of interest left in me—the pride I had in this young girl. She was so exquisitely beautiful that her presence created a sensation wherever she appeared. She began to make acqaintances; first of school girls of her own age, and soon after, of their brothers and friends. Of evenings she filled the parlors with her company. Mrs. Kneeland, our landlady, was as much interested in Emma's visitors as Emma was, and assisted in entertaining them. Emma's contributions to social life consisted in being beautiful, and in laughing musically, and in listening with the sweetest and most genial interest to those who were willing to do the talking. Old and young worshiped her; and before our year in that place was out I firmly believe she had twenty offers of marriage from young men, middle-aged men, old men and boys.

She was unwilling to go down into the parlors of an evening without me, and so I was often with her there, trying my best to add to her happiness in every way I could. I do not know why it did not occur to me to marry Emma to some one of her eligible suitors, and thus provide a home for her as well as myself; but I did not seem to think of it, though I despised to have to earn my living by teaching, and it was the only thing I could do. I cannot recall what kind of ideas I had about marriage in those days. I am sure I had not gotten over the belief born in me that marriage was the only hope life held out to any woman; neither was I forgetful of the fact that time was slipping along with me, and that I was beginning to be considered Emma's "old-maid" sister. I must have been between twenty-three and twenty-four.

As the days went on, Emma and I seemed to become very popular. The best people in the place, young and old, visited us; invitations were showered upon us, and every available moment we could spare—I from my school duties and Emma from her studies—was filled with social pleasures.

From the first evening I spent in helping "Em" entertain her "cubs," my attention had been arrested by a young medical student, of whom I often spoke to Mrs. Kneeland as the one I would rather see attached to Emma than any of the others. He had a fine pair of expressive dark eyes, and was otherwise attractive personally; but the thing which pleased me most was the quickness of his wit. Turning his gentle, but always brilliant face toward one who was talking with him, he had power to apprehend every shade of thought that arose in the person's mind; and nothing could have been more charming than his responsiveness. Then, too, he had been a great student in his college and was master of the language. I never have known anyone who always used the right word in the right place with such unerring results as he did. And he was witty beyond any person I had seen then. How he did make me laugh, and how he enjoyed his power to do so! enjoyed it the more because so few had this power; for—as I have said—I was under a cloud at the time that deadened me all over except in my love for this sweet sister of mine.

But I acknowledged the many attractions of this young man, and began to weave a romance for him and Emma. I was pleased to see him watch her as he was sitting by me, and to hear him laugh with her; for she had the kind of laugh that brings a responsive laugh from others, whether there is anything to laugh at or not. He often spoke of her beauty; and on occasions when he had gone rather long without speaking of it, I would speak of it to him.

Another season at the medical school, and he would graduate. Then his future was sure; at least, I thought so. He was undoubtedly intellectual, and his family connections were of the most desirable. What could hinder him from making Emma an excellent husband, after he had become fully equipped for the practice of medicine? He was in his twenty-second year, two years younger than I was, and seven years older than Emma.

When Emma and I were alone she talked to me of her friends, both boys and girls, and it seemed as if she was about equally interested in all of them; no more in love with this favorite of mine than with any of the others. I sometimes said to her, "Why, Emma, don't you see that Harry Washburn is the superior of the whole crowd?" To which she would give a cold, indifferent affirmative, or no answer at all. And so things slipped along; but never a day passed in which I failed to add something to the air castle I was building for Harry Washburn and Emma. Six months passed and I was still building. He was the darlingest, sweetest boy on earth; he was the only person in the world good enough and brilliant enough for my lovely little pet sister. But he did not declare himself.

One night he called, and Emma was gone; everybody was gone. I felt his disappointment and told him so before I offered him a seat. He looked at me with a kind of impatient despair in his eyes; he waited a moment and I could feel the gathering of resolution in him until the atmosphere vibrated with a force that was new to me. He crossed the room to the lounge.

"Come here, Miss Wilmans," he said, "I want to see you, and I am glad that Emma is out. Now, tell me, if you please, whether or not you have a separate existence from that little sister of yours, or if you are simply the tail to her kite and expect to remain so all your life?"

I answered truly that I had not the least idea what he was talking about.

"There is no reason why you should not understand me; and my actions have been plain enough. There are none so blind as those who won't see."

"But, Harry, I think I have seen all along. Now speak out; for nothing but words will clinch matters when they come to a climax."

"Yes I *will* speak out. I love *you*, Miss Wilmans, and I never loved another girl in my life. I saw your sister first, and was drawn into her train by her wonderful beauty. I had spent several evenings with her before I met you. I tried to reason myself into believing I was in love with her; I asked myself how it was possible not to be in love with her; but my self-questioning was knocked into the middle of next year the very first time I saw you. When I went home from here that night 'I walked on thrones.' I had never known what life was before. I was alive for the first time. And what am I to think of the fact that you have never seen it, never even dreamed of what I was feeling? If affection like mine can exist and awaken no response, I want to know what you are made of? There is not a guest that frequents this house who does not know it. The very walls and furniture of these rooms are permeated with the fact, and if an essence could be extracted from them, as it is extracted from roses, it would be pure attar of love."

Oh! the glow of the boy's eyes; and the extravagance of his language as—driven by his impetuosity—he poured out the liquid fire of his young passion upon me. Yet, all the time, mingled with his confession—there ran a thread of reproach because I had not known; and in some insidious way he made me feel that in comparison with him I was nothing but a lump of putty. He did not mean to do this, but he did it. He sat there on the lounge quite apart from me; his attitude was calm, but I could see that his muscles were vibrant with positiveness. The brilliancy of his dark eyes was gloomed over as if under a cloud, and the baleful gleams that broke through the shadows tore their way through my sympathies and pained me intensely.

But there was more than sympathy in my feelings as I continued to listen. Slowly and by almost imperceptible degrees, the very atoms of my body became winged, and arose trembling beneath the force of his words. Yes, trembling and poised, ready to meet the touch of his lips, the clasp of his arms.

But he did not know this. Filled with disappointment because I had assigned him to Emma, he could not imagine the rapid transference in my mind from her to me, and he went away with his head bowed and with tears in his eyes; but with a step as firm and a manner as manly as ever; yes, more so; for that night was the first time I had particularly observed the self-poise of his beautiful body, and the splendid dignity of his carriage.

CHAPTER XIV.

"FEARFULLY" IN LOVE.

One cannot always be writing love scenes, and I suppose I ought to hasten on with this narrative and leave the readers to guess the outcome. They already know that I did not marry my boy lover; but they cannot know what an awakening of the emotional nature it was for me, nor how it literally tore my soul in pieces, and darkened my life for years after.

The emotional nature is the torture chamber of the human organism. That is, it is the torture chamber to one who *lives* in it. It is an essential part of the human being; it is that part which generates warmth, passion, but it will not do for this part to dominate the intellect. Its true function is to furnish motive power—steam—for the intellect, but it is not the home of the intellect, nor the master of it, but its servant and slave.

And yet we live in this part of ourselves when we are young, and it tortures us while it governs us; and, indeed, under the law of growth, every atom of it is in conspiracy with every other atom to force us to move forward to the upper story of pure reason, and leave the steam-generating department to its legitimate business of furnishing force for the brain.

It was several days before I saw Harry again. In the meantime I was in such a strain of anxiety that the action of my heart ran down below zero. Every thought I could generate flowed toward him, until I was in a condition of depletion bordering on collapse.

The interpretation of the above paragraph is—that I was "fearfully" in love. I had given myself away completely. This is what being in love means to a person who has been through the experience and comes out of it with enough intelligence left to reason on the situation with any degree of correctness.

Being in love is nothing less than the temporary abandonment of self; the merging of the self in another; and anything more distressing than it is while it lasts—taking into consideration its anxieties as they alternate with its hopes—I can get no conception of. The sudden transitions from heaven to hell, the rapidity of the ascents and descents, were too much for my patient endurance; and even while I was enslaved by the feeling, I resented its tyranny, though I did not or could not free myself from it.

I recognized even then that it was a condition which darkened, instead of illuminating the intelligence; a condition that rendered cool, calm, sensible judgment impossible—thus making marriage—the one institution founded upon it—the most uncertain venture that men and women can undertake.

Why, what is it but a fever of the blood, which burns itself out in time, leaving too often nothing but ashes? What is it but a mighty stimulant which, like other stimulants, first lifts to the seventh heaven of happiness, and then prostrates to the lowest depths in reaction?

Nevertheless the belief in it is widespread as the race, and I hardly dare write my convictions concerning it. Nine-tenths of all the literature in the world are founded in a belief—not only of the power of this mighty emotion to rule mankind, but of its right to do so. Millions of unsophisticated souls are ready to shout a negation to every word I can say against it; though, indeed, I have nothing to say against it in itself, since it is a part of the human organism that cannot be dispensed with; but I have much to say against the position assigned it as ruler in the affairs of life. It is a usurper. The intellect is, or should be, master, and the love nature should be subordinate to it.

Otherwise it runs away with us and makes fools of us. I do not expect to convince many persons of the folly of being governed by the emotions. The race is young yet, and it has not suffered enough to believe what I am saying; or rather, perhaps, the experiences derived from the emotions are too seductive in spite of their painfulness to cause people to investigate their true office in the human body and to subordinate them to their proper place. But I shall give something of my own experience; and if there happens to be even a small number among my readers, who are able to take the hint and forever refuse to be enslaved by so brainless a thing as the emotion which is well described when spoken of as the condition of having "*fallen* in love," then I shall have done some good; while at the same time it need not destroy the faith of thousands of its victims who are not ready to break their allegiance to it.

It is the truth that after four or five days of this life outflow towards Harry, I was not only weakened physically all over, but mentally also. I am sure of it, because the strong, self-poised expression of my face had degenerated into one of almost maudlin idiocy. What is there in life to compensate for such complete loss of the self as this? Does the ownership of another, as in marriage, do it? No, it does not; but this ownership kills it, and releases the brain to its normal action again; and this is the best thing 1 can say of marriage. It is the death of emotional love.

But because I did not marry my boy lover, the cords of my affections reaching out to him were not broken for years and years after we had parted.

It was on the fifth evening after he had declared his love for me, and I was constantly absorbed in the thought of another visit from him, when I heard the tinkle of a guitar beneath my window. I was leaning out of this window in the most lackadaisical attitude when the sound reached me. The night was as dark as pitch, and the weather was at its hottest. My room was dark also except for the faint glimmer of a small lamp in the adjoining hall. Presently he sang, and I recognized his voice. It was not a remarkable voice for singing, though its conversational tone was manly and strong; a deep, rich bass, whose power I had not known until I heard it break—for a moment only—into almost a sob that night in which he spoke of his love.

It was Harry again after the lapse of ages—to me. It was light after almost interminable darkness. He sang that old song—new then:

" 'Tis but an hour since first we met,
Another and our barks may sever."

The words were unwisely chosen and filled me with pain. If the crack of doom had rent the air it could not have startled my quivering heart more terribly. What an extravagant young fool I was! The idea of parting forever after having once met him was death.

The song finished I think he moved away. My heart turned to palpable lead within my breast. My head fell on my arms as they rested on the casement. I must have been near fainting, for I did not hear him return; but I heard the guitar again, and then these words:

"I know an eye so softly bright,
That glistens like a star at night;
My soul it draws with glances kind.
To heaven's blue vault, and there I find
Another star as pure and clear
As that which mildly sparkles here.
Beloved eye, beloved star,
Thou art so near and yet so far.
If closed at last that radiant eye should be,
No more the day will dawn for me;
If night should dim its laughing light
Oh! then forever, ever 'twill be night.
Those eyes that brightly, softly shine
For me the sun and moon combine!
Beloved eye, beloved star,
Thou art so near and yet so far."

As this last song was proceeding, it came to me that I had not given him a word of encouragement

on that last evening, though I had so longed to do it;
and that he was really in a very hopeless state. This
view of the matter toned me up to my normal condition, and made me decide that my best plan would
be to strengthen his courage in pursuit of my
affections.

I found myself laughing; for with the thought of
strengthening his courage, I caught sight, in imagination, of little Em as I had seen her a week before,
sitting on the piano stool and telling an anecdote that
was meant to have some reference to me as I had
appeared in a game of ball that day.

It was about a woman who lived at Cape Cod, where
the wind blows pretty much all the time, and where
from the occupation of the people as fishermen, the
children knew many nautical phrases and the correct
way of applying them.

This particular woman, who was very fat, Em
assured us, "even fatter than Helen," had a son Bill
that she was in the habit of correcting provided she
could catch him. One day Bill had committed some
outrage, and ran through the open door and down
the beach for dear life, with his mother in full chase,
and rapidly gaining on him under the favoring circumstances of full sail and the wind behind her.

Another urchin standing near, perceiving how the matter was going, roared out, "Try her on the wind, Bill." No sooner said than done. Bill swung his small craft around, and sailed into the very teeth of the gale, while his mother went to leeward like a log.

Laughing quite like my old self, I leaned out of the window as the song ceased and said,

"Harry, do you remember that anecdote Emma told the other evening?"

"No, I don't."

"I do. The gist of it was, 'Try her on the wind, Bill.'"

There was a momentary silence, and then Harry spoke again manfully, peremptorily, yet with a laugh in his tones.

"You come down here, Miss Wilmans, immediately if not sooner."

"And you go to the parlors, Harry, and light up."

And oh! what an evening that was. Emma was away and we two lovers were alone. I never forgot it; and years afterwards I found that the remembrance of it was as vivid with Harry as with me.

It was the beginning of the most virulent mixture of heaven and hell that ever poisoned two lives. I really think that I never was happy when under the influence of this love, unless those moments of temporary release from some almost unbearable pain arising from it, could be called happiness. I never, except for a few hours at a time, rested on his assurance of love, but kept feeling that it was too good to be true, and that such blessedness could not possibly exist for me.

This feeling destroyed the fun-loving spirit in me and made me sombre and melancholly. I was so changed that I am sure his admiration must have abated somewhat, and with this abatement he began to be attracted to other girls who were jollier than I was. With half the knowledge of human nature that I now have I could have kept him true as steel. I could have made myself irresistible by simply developing myself in the direction of his taste. He wanted me to be brilliant and witty, and also to keep up with the literature of the time. It was this in me that had caught his fancy and captured his affections; and when I turned dull and sombre he was perplexed, at least, and probably disappointed, so that he began to look out for these same qualities in others.

Yet all the time there was a tenderness about him that was for me alone. Years of devotion that followed stand in proof of what I have just written.

He never got over his love for me while he lived. But during the months of which I am writing he did not understand me; he did not know how greatly I stood in fear of losing him; and it was in consequence of this fear that I did lose him finally.

He was so attractive that almost every one sought him. He was so kind-hearted and generous and had such a faculty for knowing how to do everything that needed to be done. If a window shade in the parlor was refractory he fixed it; if the pictures were not arranged artistically he could not stand them, but hunted the stepladder, and such other things as were necessary, and made the change.

Wherever he was he drew people to him. At the depot he was the centre point toward which all the perplexed female tribe gravitated with irresistible force. He bought their tickets, and explained the route, and had trunks checked, and made everything and everybody all right. His bright, handsome face was everywhere whenever help was needed. At the dances and picnics he was just as useful and as pleasant.

He seemed to love everybody. I thought he loved some of them too much, and sulked about it. He did not know what ailed me when I was sulking, and fancied that my love was cooling and was repelled, and no doubt grieved. But his patience was indefatigable, and he bore all my moods with gentleness.

I did not know him, and I did not know how to love rationally. Indeed, I did not know anything about the matter then, and I do not yet; only "good Lord, deliver me" from ever having another experience of the kind. My emotional nature was too strong to bear such a complete upsetment at a time when my intellect had not become strong enough to control it. And so I tore myself to pieces daily, and I know I must have brought more pain than pleasure to the gentle heart of my boy lover.

I have been a great novel reader in my time; and never yet have I seen the passion of love portrayed more powerfully than I felt it, and never have I read such portrayal but the old feeling has come back to tear at my heart with the same irresistible force.

This talk of the "heights of ecstasy" connected with this passion may be true for others, but I must confess I never was there, and the sentence does not "palpitate with actuality" for me. Like Huck Finn, when he read "Pilgrim's Progress," the descriptions of the thing "are interestin' but tough," and no experience of mine can corroborate them.

Falling in love seems to be a falling down below the ordinary action of the every-day brain. It is a surrendery of the brain to a power which should be held in abeyance; and in this way it is a reversal of the position that has made man—in the process of evolution—an upright creature. At least, this is my belief to-day; but I reserve the privilege of changing my opinion on the subject if ever more light comes; that is, if I ever "fall in love" again. Here is a chance for that irrepressible "small fry" up in Boston to laugh. The idea of grandmamma's falling in love!

There were times when I harbored the thought of breaking with Harry, out of my intense longing for freedom; but I could not do it. And the year wore on and the time came for us both to leave; I for my brother's home in Cedar Rapids, and he for his last term in the Chicago medical school; and so we parted.

I seem to be psychologized by this recital. I am taken back through the pain of the whole thing once more. My heart feels like lead in my breast, and my hand is too nerveless to write.

There happened to be some new ideas in medical matters coming to the front at that time, and Gus being a progressive man wanted to go to Chicago for a brief season of study, and there he met Harry.

I do not know how Gus could keep from loving Harry, but he did not love him, though Harry was more than kind to him, and tried in every way to win his favor. It is true that Harry went into society that he should have avoided, and that he was often under the influence of drink; but I believe that Gus could have kept him straight if he had tried. As it was, Gus became more and more angry to think of my marrying him, and treated him shamefully at last. How I was included in the breach I cannot recall, but it is certain that I was included, and that our letters grew cold, especially his, until at last it was all over.

I will not attempt to describe in detail how I felt; but it is an actual fact that the light of the whole world went out for me, and only began to come back when my first baby was laid in my arms some two years later.

One evening, about three months after my break with Harry, as I sat in the parlor alone, it being late and the family in bed, there came a ring at the door. As Gus had calls all times of the night I thought nothing of it, as I answered the bell. I opened the parlor door into the hall and stepped to the hall door. In opening the hall door the parlor door swung shut, leaving me in black darkness; but the person outside had caught a momentary glimpse of me before the light was shut off. I could not see even the faintest outlines of him, but he spoke my name, "Helen," and I knew his voice.

"Dr. Baker," I said, and the next moment the big, strong fellow had me in his arms.

We went into the lighted parlor and looked at each other. Seven years had passed and he was trenching on middle age, but he showed no sign of it. He was splendidly dressed, and was a splendid looking man. I knew even before he spoke that he intended to marry me, and I knew that I was too heart-broken and too weak, both physically and mentally, to resist.

Nevertheless I did resist to the extent of telling him all I had gone through, and how I still felt towards Harry. But he set it aside so persistently and with such firmness that at length I yielded, and with Gus's approval we were married.

Lib was married several months before I was. After my marriage it was decided that Emma should be put in a boarding school; that Lib should keep Julia, and that I was to take little Clem with me to California, where we went in a few months.

After our marriage we went back to Fairfield, where we spent a month with old friends before saying "good-bye" to them—in very many instances—forever.

There was no railroad to California then, and the steamship line had been completed but a short time. It was late in the spring of 1856 that we left New York for San Francisco. We had a storm on the Pacific and a dense fog that protracted our journey so that we were nearly four weeks on the way.

Four weeks is not a very long time even in connection with a sea voyage; but it was long enough to prove to me that I had made the biggest mistake of my life in my marriage.

CHAPTER XV.

A BROKEN IDOL.

I have not one word to say against my husband, who in many ways was a grand character. He was a man of rare integrity, and commanded the respect of other men to a very marked degree. But he was a most unhappy disposition, and looked on the dark side of life every day, and all the time, to the utter exclusion of the bright side. I think he was the most wretched and self-tormenting man I ever knew.

He took the chance of winning my affection when he married me, and he might have done it had he known how. But he began to doubt his ability to do so, and to doubt my fealty to him almost immediately and without the slightest cause. He could not bear to have me make any acquaintances on the ship; he made no effort to entertain me himself, but was cross with me because others did. We had lovely weather the first part of our voyage. The sea was like a mirror and the deck of our vessel was as level as a ball room floor. There was a fine band aboard, and we danced not only in the evenings, but often in the day time also. This dancing was one prolonged aggravation to the doctor.

I was a member of a church that forbade dancing, and yet I had broken over on more than one occasion. It was so easy for the music to get into my heels that the temptation was irresistible.

After an unusually long voyage, owing to a storm that came on after we crossed the Isthmus, we got into San Francisco early in June 1856. Here we remained but a day or two, and then went to Suisun Valley where my husband's farm was located. This is one of the richest valleys in the whole state, the soil being particularly deep, and productive beyond belief.

All my life I had despised a farm. The sounds on a farm, so pleasing to many, were lonesome and unmusical and sickening to me. The lowing of cattle, the crowing of chickens, the conversation of the ducks and geese—which I really did like when I came to understand their language—were all mere jargon to me then, and added to the inharmony which reigned within me.

The farmhouse was a miserable structure scarcely fit for a cow shed. There were no conveniences of any kind in it, and no attractions outside of it. The valley itself was simply a flat, unbroken plain with here and there a stunted oak tree. These trees were all leaning in one direction, showing the effect of the trade winds, which blew for six months out of the year in an almost unbroken gale. The sky was gray in summer with fog from the bay; the entire aspect was the acme of gloom. Out on the road—if one ventured out—the dust caused by the long dry season was swept in clouds either with or against you, so that it mattered not whether your clothes were soiled or clean when you left home.

This was the summer of that most wearisome climate. The winter was better. There was scarcely ever the slightest touch of frost. The trade winds ceased, and the gray went out of the sky, leaving it beautifully blue, except when the rains came. The rains, too, were a real delight. They were so needed; every growing thing was so covered with dust; and the cracked earth drank the descending waters greedily.

In the winter the plowing was done and the wheat planted. It was mostly wheat that we raised.

Our farm was large, and my husband was considered a rich man. He had about quit the practice of medicine and gave his entire time to his crops.

I must have been an extremely reticent girl not to have told him of my disinclination to fill the position he assigned me; a position of such slavery as would scarcely be thought possible for any woman to fill.

It took nine or ten men in the winter to get the crop in. It took from twenty to twenty-five to take it off; and the crops were so heavy that it frequently required three months to harvest them. This was before farming machinery had made the improvements in farmers' work that it has since done.

I did the cooking and the housework for this crowd of men, and my washing and ironing and sewing besides. I was up before day, and was rarely in bed before midnight. I had a few neighbors who worked as hard as I did in proportion to their strength, though none of them were half so strong as I was.

I think it took nearly two years to toughen me to the work. During this time I had wept in secret over my lonely and truly dreadful position until my eyes quite failed me and I was compelled to put on glasses.

But just before I got the glasses my baby came, and I was no longer alone.

It is true that my little sister Clem was with me during this time, but I had kept her in school; and even when she was at home I was resolved not to have her enslaved by the uncongenial work that was fast destroying the beauty of my hands and complexion, and that was already beginning to stiffen my joints somewhat.

But this baby—Ada! If I do some crowing over her I freely give every other mother the same privilege. I never saw such a baby as she was. I have never seen any other baby so precocious. Her intelligence seems marvelous now as I look back and see what she did, and later what she said, and how she performed generally. Such a madcap laugh as she had, and such appreciation of fun! The little scamp played a practical joke on me before she was six months old. I had nursed her to sleep (as I supposed) and had placed her in her crib and started out to wash the supper dishes. Hearing a joyous little squeal and a rapturous, ringing laugh behind me, I turned, and there she stood on her tiny feet holding by the railing, rippling all over with mirth, while her eyes said unmistakably that she had played a trick on me.

And yet, not thinking it possible that a baby of her age could get off a practical joke, I nursed her to sleep again. It only took about a minute this time, and I placed her in the crib and started out, to be once more arrested by that musical peal which said as plainly as spoken words, "I've fooled you again."

I now began to experiment with her, and she kept repeating the performance until at last she was overpowered by sleep.

Shortly after this she began to talk, and when she was eleven months old she put sentences together admirably.

The farm hands, many of whom were men of sterling worth and culture, and had been leading citizens before they became stranded in a new country so far from home, were very fond of her, and took almost the exclusive care of her when they were about the house.

Babies were at a premium then in California, there being but few families there. I recall the time I went to a camp meeting when she was some eight or ten months old. I could scarcely keep track of her. The men had her and were passing her around. They all wanted her, and in a little bashful, coquettish way she wanted them. Evidently she appreciated their admiration. She would be brought back to me at intervals with her little fat paws full of gold nuggets and gold coins that they gave her.

She learned to read almost as soon as she could

talk. The men taught her the letters from newspapers at nights and on Sundays; and it was the richest thing I ever saw to witness her attempts at spelling and pronouncing the difficult words. They said she had "the grit to buck at anything;" and they taxed their ingenuity to find words long enough and hard enough. With her brilliant, laughing eyes she would watch them for each fresh word, and start into it with a rush of letters and a jumble of syllables that usually culminated in a vortex wherein the word itself was frequently overwhelmed, or only a faint semblance of it escaped; and the effort would be followed by her little, wild, reckless laugh, with such a ring of high vitality, that we were drawn into it irresistibly. Such fun as we had with the bright thing!

When she was three years old the men were in the habit of setting her on a large table of an evening while she read the newspapers aloud to them. I scarcely owned the child at all..

Those were primitive times in California. It was nothing to ride ten miles to a dance, and take her along. Indeed, before she was two years old she had a baby sister who was with her in all her excursions.

Riding up to the school house—we usually held our

dances in the school houses sparsely scattered over the country—it not unfrequently chanced that twenty or thirty of the neighbors would be there to help us to dismount. My husband did not like to have me go to these dances, and often refused to accompany me. But there were always plenty of others who were willing to take care of us, and I would not be altogether restrained. Nearly all the women in a radius of fifteen miles would be there with their children. Beds were extemporized for the little ones out of saddle blankets and shawls, and the surplus men who could not dance took care of them when they needed care. Babies were passed around from one person to another, and no person seemed to feel them a burden. As for my volatile little tow-head she scarcely slept at all, but threw herself into the music and let the music dance her baby feet the whole night long. "And we didn't go home till morning."

But on the tiresome ride home I had time for reflection. I expected to meet scowls, and they never failed me. Always before going to one of these dances I would make such perfect preparations for breakfast that there was scarcely anything to do besides steeping the coffee, and some of the men were always willing to do this for me. So that my going did not upset my household work. But that I would go at all vexed my husband, and he had very little consideration as to the way he manifested his feelings. He had his views of a wife's duties, and they would have enslaved me completely if I had complied with them perfectly.. I did comply with them entirely too much. I worked too hard. It would scarcely be believed that one woman could do the work that I did. In the twenty years I lived with him, less than two years would cover the time I had any household help. I showed him my swollen and stiffened joints, and told him I could not stand it to work so hard. But he only kept promising that when he got out of debt I should have help all the time. I knew quite well that if he had had my work to do, or a similar amount of work of another kind, that he would have hired two or more men to do it without reference to getting out of debt. But I had not sufficient positiveness to assert myself, and so I bore it; not without complaining and making things quite lively for short intervals, however.

If I had been brought up with any other idea than that of man's God-given right to lord it over woman, I could have changed the whole tenor of my life and of his also. Knowing him as well as I did later, I am sure I could have taken the management of the business in my own hands, and with small opposition on his part. I think, too, I could have made a success of it. One thing certain, it would not have been possible to botch it worse than it was botched.

It was his complete lack of business ability that kept him in hot water. He should never have abandoned his profession for farming. In his profession he was at the head, and he passed for his full worth. Sixteen dollars a visit was a doctor's regular price for attendance on patients. Up to the time he bought the farm he had a large practice. He was known and trusted all over that part of the state.

A practicing physician's duties are hard, and he was tired of them. So he bought land. After his first purchase of two hundred acres of the richest land I ever saw, he began to want more. He wanted all the land that bordered on his land. In short, he wanted the world. He kept purchasing until he had invested all his money, and still he kept purchasing.

Interest on money in California at that time was three per cent. a month. Land did not go up as rapidly as he expected. It did not go up at all. The crops were large, but prices varied so that no one knew when to sell. The doctor never was satisfied with a fair paying price, but usually held his grain until the market had touched the highest point and tumbled over the edge down and down toward nothingness.

No wonder he was filled with anxiety, and that he did not understand how I could canter off ten miles to a dance with a baby in my lap, and another one in the lap of one of the neighbors. He thought me indifferent to his troubles. He did not know that the gloom of his face had become a perpetual terror to me, and that my heart quailed whenever I heard his step on the porch.

His entire attitude repelled me. He was not only unhappy, but he was irritable. He did not mean to be unkind, and he was not really so; but he often said things inadvertently that made me cry for hours. His indifference to the fact of my working so hard was a growing hurt, and I came in time to almost hate him for it.

I could not forget that I had once been loved; and the recollection of Harry Washburn was with me almost hourly. I discovered later that it was not Harry to whom I was true, but an ideal that Harry failed utterly to fill. I had not stood in the same mental tracks all these years; I had been growing; and I had outgrown Harry, but I did not know it until after I met him again and saw him as he really was.

My two young daughters were growing towards womanhood, and where I lived there were no educational advantages. I should have said before this that the interest the doctor was paying on money had compelled him to sell his land where we had been living. Only a few thousand dollars were left us; and with this sum we went to the mountains of Lake county, a wild and beautiful spot, and there began to raise stock. Our family consisted of the two daughters I have spoken of, and one son, Claude, and baby Jenny; the most angelic little girl I ever saw. She only lived to be nine years old, but she left a void never to be filled.

I could not rest and feel that Ada and Florence were growing up without the advantages of a thorough education, and so I resolved to take them to San Francisco and put them into a good school. This determination of mine met with much resistance from the doctor, but I would not be overruled. The matter was too important. I had sacrificed everything to his belief in the power of poverty—even my health and strength, and such measure of beauty as I had possessed; but I would go no farther. So I had my way.

I firmly believed that if I had the time for writing I could earn enough for the family support. My experiences in this attempt will be recorded in another chapter. I reached San Francisco all right; and no bird freed from its cage ever felt such an upliftment as I did. I met my old friends, the Daltons, here, and they assisted me in finding a suitable house and in becoming settled.

I knew that Harry was in San Francisco, because it had been announced in the papers several years before. He had become a distinguished man, and was high up in a literary position which his own ability— such as it was—had established for him.

I had made no effort to find him, and secretly dreaded a meeting with him. I know of nothing more distressing than the constant crushing which goes on among the hard-working farmers' wives, whereby they come to habitually distrust themselves, until they fear to face any but their commonest acquaintances.

Such an intense timidity was on me all the time that I am sure I would have gone on secretly dreaming of Harry to the end of my days, without ever giving him a sign of my presence, had not fate or

accident or the law of attraction ordered otherwise.
I was on Kearney street one day with Jenny. She
was about four years old; and I recall how beautiful
she looked as she ran ahead of me with her fluffy curls
trying to keep up with her, and in their grace and
lightness only settling on her fair shoulders a moment
at a time, then rising again to be borne on the air
behind her—Oh, my baby!

The day was delicious and I felt as joyous as a girl.
It seemed as if I might let Harry know of my presence
in the city, and give him a chance to see me if he
wished to. I felt quite sure that he would not want
to see me; but the rest I had by this time taken from
hard work, with the addition of a few fashionable
garments, had greatly added to my self-possession, so
that I was less timid than formerly.

Absorbed in a delightfully hopeful revery, and
watching Jenny with loving eyes, I scarcely noticed a
man who passed me rapidly, and turned and passed
me again. I caught his eye in full as we met face to
face; I knew it was Harry, almost unchanged and
handsomer than ever. But I gave him no look of
recognition, for I think I had turned to stone, and he
passed behind me once more. Then he repeated the
same performance; but in the hasty flash of his dis-

appearance I made up my mind that I would not recognize him. All my pride came in a rush. I was so changed, while in him the change was for the better. Heavens, how this matter chilled me! It removed me from the warm atmosphere in which my thoughts had been dwelling, and sent me to some North-pole mental condition where I was frozen to death, but still conscious of my own womanly dignity and worth.

But he was not to be resisted. On coming again face to face with me he grasped my hands in unmistakable welcome. Then Jenny who was the most friendly little thing that ever was, perceiving her mother's new acquaintance, caught him around the knees and with her upturned, smiling face danced a little welcome on his toes and the adjoining pavement.

He looked down and then laughed his old genial, happy laugh. "It's *your* baby, Helen," he said, and caught her up and kissed her rapturously. And then he began to talk.

"I have no children, though I have wished for them much. My sisters have enough, and in each family there is a Helen because I desired it. I have perpetuated your name right and left, even if I have no little Helen of my own."

He told me among other things that he would have known me in China; that I was not greatly changed, etc.

But to end this matter and this chapter. I will only add that I exchanged visits frequently with him and his lovely wife; that before I had been with them much, I liked her better than I did him. For it is a fact that he had made no advancement in his ideas at all, and was one of the most conservative men alive; weakly so; conservative to a degree that made him appear intrinsically unmanly. His success in life had sprung greatly from this fact. His fine literary education, together with his rare command of language, had made him a mouth piece through the public prints for the aristocratic element of the city; and his sentiments bore hard upon my own awakening ideas of justice as administered there and then.

It did not take me long to find out that I had not been loving Harry all these years, but like a vast number of married women and men too, whose marriages have proven fearfully uncongenial, I had simply been holding an ideal of what might have been.

CHAPTER XVI.

THE FETTERS ARE FALLING.

After about two years in San Francisco, much of which time Dr. Baker spent with me quite pleasantly, I returned to the ranch. A little later Harry died. A letter from his wife gave me all the particulars. She was quite heart-broken; but the event did not bring a tear from me. He had gone out of my life before this as completely as if I had never known him.

As before mentioned, the reason of this lay in the fact that I had been growing mentally, while he had not. I had passed above and beyond the habitual range of his ideas. The hard lessons of my life had been educating me, while he—lacking such teachers—missed the education.

I had *thought* myself out of the church; out of all belief in a personal God; out of the Bible account of creation into the evolutionary theory; and I was investigating every idea that promised to lead in the direction of truth. The very moment we touched upon any of these subjects we clashed; and presently there was nothing for us to talk about, and his presence would tire me.

It was not a matter of surprise to me that he succeeded in literature where I had failed. He was able to give the reading public the kind of pap it demanded; the food I tried to cram down its throat was too strong for it, and was rejected by it. Then, too, it was immensely in his favor that he was a practiced writer and a master of composition. I had ideas without any adequate medium of expression. He had no ideas, and wrote brilliant and beautiful nothings that had a tendency to please the average reader without antagonizing him, and also without arousing a thought. He was just the man for his position, and drew his princely salary from the largest moneyed corporation on the Pacific coast. He was a stool pidgeon in the hands of a conscienceless gang of millionaires, who, through the newspapers they had subsidized, sought to amuse the public while they robbed it.

And he could do this under the benignant smile of the God he worshiped, and rail at me for having departed from his infantile religious beliefs. No wonder he became tiresome.

And now I will go back awhile and tell how I got out of the religious beliefs I was born into.

And I say boldly and in defiance of all Christendom that the combined ills which prey upon the race and hold it in the slavery of ignorance are as nothing in comparison with its religious beliefs. Religion is the foundation rock on which rests every trouble and sorrow that besets humanity. It is organized in the belief of man's inherent weakness; it fosters his belief in his own nothingness; its entire tendency is to develop *things* and not *men*.

Religion has not one solitary particle of true logic on which to rest. It was born of ignorance, bolstered by superstition, fed by that bugaboo of the ages, "authority."

And an utterly baseless authority at that; an authority that cannot rise higher than the understanding of man, or it would lose its connection with him, and fail to be available even for purposes of self-delusion.

Religion was born at a time when the understanding of man was scarcely higher than that of the apes. It fastened itself upon the ignorant wonder of his questioning faculties and took possession of them.

That religion has been an essential incident in

race growth I am not going to deny. That it was a necessity of race growth to go through the stultifying process in order that it might learn the true way from the false, I shall not deny. Truth always—in our development—presents its negative pole to us first; that is, it shows us first what is not true, and from this point of observation we gradually feel our way toward what is true.

Thus, religion that endeavors to teach man his weakness, leads him through experiences that would ruin him if they did not direct him to the very reverse of what they teach, and finally show him his strength.

The very moment a man begins to live from a consciousness of his own strength he sees small use of a personal God; his reasoning powers awake, and little by little he reverses the entire scheme and comes out on top. Inasmuch as he had been a slave under his belief in the supremacy of a personal God, he sees himself the governing power and the creative force of the world, with the Principle of Being at his service and *under his command.* And oh! what a change this is.

The religious superstition hung heavily upon my mind and heart always. Even in my happiest hours I felt it an ever present weight below the surface of my gayety. I was never quite free from it. But it was only when that fair, little, downy-ball of intense vitality—my baby—came to my arms that I began to be actively wretched about the doctrines of my church. It was then that the horrors of future punishment fastened cruel tentacles in my very flesh and made me wild with anxiety. I had borne these thoughts so far as I myself was concerned with some degree of fortitude. For, indeed, it seemed that my own salvation rested with myself to a certain degree. Except in the matter of dancing I was faithful in all religious observances. I attended church regularly and reverently. I gave money for the support of the gospel with a liberal hand. I saved it up in every way I could; I took it from my housekeeping expenses, and from the sale of my poultry; and denied myself almost everything in order to do it. I kept open house for all the preachers in that part of the country, and was imposed upon to an almost unlimited extent by them.

It will be wondered what my husband was thinking about during this time. I must confess that he was acting the perfect gentleman. He was humoring me in my beliefs. Never in all his life had he been for one moment under the influence of any religious opinions. Still he considered it no part of his right

to interfere with me in this matter. He was a man—
who having formed his own opinion of right and
wrong—could hold to his conclusion rigidly.

He sometimes asked me questions about certain
hopelessly unreasonable tenets held by my religion,
and smiled cynically at my answers; but beyond this
he let me alone. He usually went with me to church,
and frequently returned in a very bad temper. Still
on the whole I am sure he behaved much better than
I would have done had our positions been reversed.

What in the world is sweeter than a baby girl except two baby girls? When Ada was four years old
and Florence a trifle over half that, they were the
same size, and were taken for twins. They were in
the habit of trudging about holding each other by the
hand, and talking together in one unbroken stream of
talk, interspersed with such ripples and cascades of
laughter as I had never heard before.

What wonder that the thought of their salvation
from sin, and their eternal happiness was forced upon
me? I saw that my own salvation would not save
them, and that according to the tenets of my church
I might come to the place of eternal parting with
them. This thought was not so unbearable as it
would have been but for one much worse; the thought

that they might be everlastingly lost; everlastingly subject to the tortures of an orthodox hell.

The horror of this kind of thinking grew on me and tortured me constantly. It robbed me of all pleasure in my children. I could better have borne to see them dead in their innocence, than to have them grow up with the certainty of hell before them, as the reward of sins so easily committed as they appeared to be.

I began to talk to the preachers who frequented our house, but failed to arouse any special interest in them. This surprised me at first, for I had foolishly imagined that they carried these infinitely important matters upon their brains and consciences every waking hour of their lives. It had seemed to me that their only mission was to "snatch souls as brands from the burning," and I was entirely unprepared for their indifference. I myself, infused by a conception of the awfulness of the situation, had become a tremendous evangelist in a limited, home-like way. I talked to the hired men with such earnestness and interest that I made converts of them in spite of the superior reasoning powers of many of them. I expect I frightened them. At all events I made church members of some of them.

I talked to everybody who would listen. I must have been an intolerable nuisance to the neighbors, many of whom did really begin to avoid the house.

And at length the preachers began to avoid me too. I "out-Heroded Herod" to such an extent that they could not stand me. I reproached them for their "lukewarmness;" I "whacked" them over the head with whole bundles of quotations from the Bible; and frequently I became personally offensive, and called them names, such as backslider, hypocrite, etc.

"How can the salvation of these babies be insured; answer me that." This was the burden of my question and my demand. Not that it was my own babies alone that agitated me. The whole race of babies and their parents included had become my own babies since my induction into motherhood.

"Oh, you cold-blooded sneaks, sailing under the garb of Christ, and satisfied to eat and sleep and wear fine clothes and do nothing, when nine-tenths of the people are on the down grade, slanting directly into the yawning mouth of hell! What do you think you are for anyhow?"

This is the question I put to four of the preachers, including the Elder, one Sunday afternoon when they were strutting about the floor, smoking cigars and discussing church gossip. The Elder turned on me.

"Sister," he said "into what condition are you drifting? How can you justify yourself in saying such things as you have been saying? The habit of insulting God's chosen servants has been growing on you of late, so that you are becoming a torment to us instead of the blessing you once were. Kneel down right here and let us pray for you."

Pray for me indeed! No words were ever spoken that let so much light into my mind on the subject of prayer. I thought of how my life had been one almost unbroken prayer, and how never a petition had been answered. Strange that I had not considered this fact before; but I never had. I saw it now plain enough.

"You shall not pray for me," I said; "you shall tell me how my children are to be saved from hell."

"Sister," replied the Elder, "be patient; have faith; make *your own* calling and election sure, and leave the fate of your children in the hands of God. I fully believe that God will save the children of such a mother as you are."

"But will all be saved? I want to know this."

"No, surely not," he answered. "Those who do not accept the gospel of Jesus Christ and believe it and live it will be damned."

"Suppose their brains are so constructed that they can't believe it?"

"Yet surely, sister, they must be damned; otherwise the words of the gospel are null and void."

"Get out of this house," I said. My voice was so low I only just heard it myself; yet every one in the room heard it distinctly. The doctor had been tilted back against the wall in a splint-bottomed chair, and his hat lay on the floor beside him. He reached down and, picking it up, placed it on his head at an angle that quite concealed his face. Otherwise he was perfectly still. All the preachers looked at me aghast and speechless. Not one of them moved.

Their hats and canes and umbrellas lay around promiscuously. My muscles quivered like the finest steel springs, so permeated were they with my thought as I picked up each separate article and pitched it out of doors. I might have been a butterfly poised in mid aid, or touching first one flower and then another, I felt so light and so superbly reckless. It was in this act that I laid down the burden of a life time, though at the moment I did not know it.

The preachers huddled out in confusion; the doctor brought the front legs of his chair to the floor and walked leisurely out. He assisted them in picking up their scattered property, and walked down the road with them. It was two hours before he returned, and in that time I had passed through a revolution.

I sat down in expectation of being overwhelmed with regret. I waited for it. It did not come. I had not dared investigate my feelings, but when at length I turned my thoughts inward I felt the strangest jubilation I ever experienced. The load of a life time was gone. What did it mean? I could no longer keep my seat. I stood up and felt no weight. It came to me that I was suddenly translated. I walked to the door to meet the same dismal and forlorn view that had shocked my sense of beauty so often; yet there was no denying the fact that I seemed to be walking on air. My load was gone, and this that I was experiencing was the first effects of freedom.

I thought of the two little girls taking their afternoon sleep in the next room. I had always been told that if I committed any unpardonable sin the first effect would show itself in the death of my mother love. But oh! what a rush of affection overwhelmed me as I looked at them. I would have waked them with my caresses, but was held back by my desire to think out the strangeness of the whole occurrence.

But how long it was before emotion gave place to

the power of thought! Indeed, it did not do so for days. For days I was filled with nothing but the jubilant sense of freedom. I quit trying to think, and felt that I could wait; and I had the assurance that thought—when it should come—would justify me.

I hardly know how long it was before the whole truth of the matter unraveled itself to my comprehension. But when it finally did so I knew that I— my own individualized intelligence—had never believed one word of the whole gospel scheme. I knew that my entire belief in it had been hypnotic. It was the world's belief sweeping over me and through me, dimming and blinding my own reasoning powers. Little by little my reasoning powers crept out from under this deadening influence and asserted themselves, and I began to be a thinking creature with vested rights of my own. I was born into a new world. Like the young plant I had burst the soil that lay so heavily above my head, and had come through into the realm of light above.

I had heard it said that when a repentant sinner "got religion" he knew it by the expansion of his love nature; that it would induct him into a feeling of love for everybody. Whether this is so or not I cannot say; but I am sure that when I *got rid* of my religion I came into this feeling with great force. I loved every living soul; even the animals and plants came in for a large share. I was so happy I can hardly convey an idea of it.

It is surprising how little we know of our neighbors until a change of position brings us into new relations with them. On the farm south of us there was a man who seemed to live particularly secluded; and the same may be said of his entire family. Nobody knew what the religious sentiments of the family were, and nobody seemed to care. They were straight-forward, honest people and gave no one any trouble.

The news of my unexampled treatment of the preachers traversed the neighborhood like wildfire, and reached this person, whose name was John Berber. The school master—a man of great learning—had boarded with Mr. Berber for years. No one knew any more of the schoolmaster's religion than of Mr. Berber's. But in less than a week after my escapade these two gentlemen came to see me. They were both perfectly independent in their religious views, and held very broad opinions on many subjects. They were deeply versed in the sciences, and were in every way unusually wise men, as well as genial, just and humorous. They gave me Paine's "Age of Reason" to read; and the unshakable arguments of that splendid book never left my mind.

But it was not in me to stand still, content with the mere denial of religion. The claims of religion were false, but there was truth somewhere and I must have it. Simply to have the terror of hell destroyed, and the whole absurd scheme of salvation exploded did not satisfy long. I was hungry for more knowledge, and could not rest without it.

As if in answer to my desire an old man who lived in the Montezuma hills, about twenty miles away from our house, got caught in the rain one evening in passing and had to remain all night. He was a Swedenborgian, and he talked Swedenborgian religion until midnight.

After that he lent me Swedenborg's books, of which there seemed to be an almost endless quantity, and I began to study them.

I studied them thoroughly, bending my whole mind to the task. It was my peculiarity to believe that every new idea I got hold of was the saving truth my soul was longing for, provided only that I could understand it thoroughly.

I will not deny that I got something out of

Swedenborg; but the best thing I got was the result of my intense application in the effort to get his system as a complete whole. The thorough bending of the mind to the accomplishment of an object always brings a big reward; and my reward came in the growth of my reasoning faculties.

I never accepted the Swedenborgian gospel in its entirety. I had become footloose and was beginning to be individualized. I was forever broken of the habit of pinning my faith to some other person's sleeve, even if that person held daily audience with the unseen powers. I was becoming indifferent to the unseen powers, and was getting a mental reef on mundane things.

CHAPTER XVII.

IN THE REFORM MOVEMENT.

All my life I had had an aspiration to become a literary woman. My efforts in this direction were numerous and my failures many and disheartening.

It is true that I had almost no time to spare from my household duties in which either to read or write, but somehow I managed to do both. I hurried through my work, stopping at intervals to run and put down an idea, until after a week or a month I had a magazine article. At least it was a magazine article until it was returned with the word "unavailable" from the publisher to whom I sent it.

This sort of thing made me sick in the beginning, but I got case-hardened after awhile, so that I was able to control my disappointment somewhat, but I cannot say that I ever enjoyed the experience.

It is a surprise to me now, in looking back, to think how I stuck to the effort in spite of the fact that so many doors were shut in my face. "Slam, bang, get out of here," seemed to be the universal attitude towards my literary aspiration. I laugh now as I think of it, but it was no laughing matter then. I laugh still more as I think of my indefatigable persistence; this is something not only to laugh about, but to be proud of. No one ever followed the life line of desire with more untiring patience than I did. Of course this perseverance had to lead me somewhere, and where could it lead me but in the direction I wanted to go; in the direction I was travelling?

After I went back to the farm from San Francisco I became very restless. Every fibre of my body and brain rebelled against the drudgery of the farm life. Hope, always strong within me, was filling me with the idea that I could write articles that would sell if I only had the time to devote to it. It was impossible to put this hope to the test while doing slave's work at least twelve hours a day.

The doctor gave me no encouragement and no sympathy. He had no hesitation in piling more and more work on me. He had discovered a vein of quicksilver on our land, and was prospecting it. So in addition to the work of the farm I had to cook for a crowd of miners. I remonstrated without avail. He seemed to consider me a machine with power to run day and night. He had consideration for his horses and for his men and for himself, but none for me. This, of course, was because I failed to define and maintain my own position. Who will say what is our due if we do not say it ourselves?

Ada and Florence at this time had gotten through the school in San Jose where I left them when I returned to the ranch from San Francisco, and were then learning the printer's trade in the town adjoining our place. So they were not far from home.

Little Jenny was dead. Claude was away at school, and I was really in a position where I could assert my freedom for the first time in my married life.

And I did assert it. The day arrived when the crowd of miners and the doctor with them came to dinner and found a cold stove and an empty house.

Directly after breakfast I had stood out in the road with a valise containing the smallest imaginable wardrobe, but all I had, waiting for some passing wagon to take me into town. I had not long to wait, and soon found myself at the boarding house of my two daughters. I had no money, and as the girls were on board wages, not having learned the trade sufficiently to earn more, I undertook the task of borrowing ten dollars to pay my expenses to the city. I ran over the town the entire day, and it was late at night before I found a friend who could let me have this small sum.

The next morning I was on the stage *en route* for San Francisco. I reached the city with $2.50 in my purse. I paid one dollar for a night's lodging and then began to search for a room. I found one in an attic that was not unpleasant, and paid my remaining $1.50 for it for one week in advance. I was not hungry, for I had the remnants of a lunch that I had brought with me from Lower Lake.

I started out to hunt a situation in some publishing house. It was three days after the last bite of my food was gone before I found a place in a printing office, where I was to superintend and write for a poor, little struggling paper at the sum of six dollars a week.

I had become so light-headed and so incapable of thinking that I barely escaped being run over in the street more than once. But I adhered to my purpose. I had said to myself many times over, "I am going to have life on my own terms, or I won't have it at all."

I was a first-class cook and housekeeper, and I could have gotten dozens of such situations, but I would not have them. I would starve first. If food served no better purpose than to nourish me in my old conditions I did not want it. And I was not hungry at all. I was cold, and felt as if I were floating, and I could not think consecutively, although I held to my resolution to keep out of housework. I had had enough of that; I would never touch it again. And in the old slavish sense I never have done so. A resolution so firm as to defy death becomes an organic thing, and takes its place among the unchangeable entities of personality in a way that no power can shake. I have established my own defense in this manner more than once, though this was the first time.

The man for whom I was working advanced me a dollar, and it sufficed until the first week's wages were paid.

Out of six dollars a week I paid the borrowed ten dollars the first thing. Then I saved up my money to bring Ada to me. In the meantime a large publisher in the next street began to notice my writings and asked me to write for one of his publications. I did so. I wrote an article for him that attracted a good deal of attention. If he had paid me as he paid his other contributors I would have received forty dollars for it. But he declined to pay for it, and promised to befriend me in other ways, such as giving my daughters each a position in his office. It was on this promise that I brought Ada to the city where she entered his employment on a good salary.

And Ada and I together soon brought Florence, and she, too, got an engagement in the same building. By this time I had resigned my poor little attic room and was in a small flat where our united wages made us very comfortable and independent and happy.

Neither was it long until I had a more remunerative position than the first one I accepted. Besides the regular salary I derived from this position, I began to sell articles to the papers and magazines; and I was rich. I will never be richer than I was then.

Bret Harte had just gone off *The Overland Monthly* as its editor when I began to write for it. It was something to write for *The Overland*. I really believe this magazine was the best representative of American thought of any other publication. It was the most vital, the most uniquely charming, the most strikingly characteristic of the entire lot of magazines. It was original; it dared be the best its editors knew in the field of literature. It did not hug any public foibles and seemed not to seek popularity as the others do.

I do not mean that it was a leader in what we call

reform work. It attempted nothing of the kind. It simply led in a fresher and more vigorous expression of literary ideas. It published articles then that the other magazines dared not publish for fear of transgressing some old preconceived opinions of literary correctness. It took a position close down to nature and became a transcription of natural people and natural thought. It waked one up as one read it, and made the heart warm with the glow of kinship in everything it contained.

Later *The Overland* passed into other hands which sought what is considered the popular vein, and it became as commonplace as the others. But at the time it was simply perfect in its way, as the representative of the fresh, vivid, young thought of a fresh, vivid, young country.

My writings were welcomed by this magazine at that time and I was well paid for them. Later—when the magazine had changed, as I have mentioned—my articles were no longer received; and, indeed, all of us pioneer writers gradually disappeared from its pages. That this change was not approved of became manifest in the falling off of its subscription list, until at one time its publication was suspended. A year or two afterwards the magazine was resurrected and placed on its feet again; but it has never exhibited any marked character of its own since.

As a writer, I came in contact with a good many minds that were considered quite brilliant, but I must say that close acquaintance rather had the effect of pushing me away instead of drawing me to them. The egotism of so many small aspirants after literary glory taught me a valuable lesson; this was to lock my own egotism carefully away and throw the key down the well.

I am not going to pretend that I had no egotism, but I do say that I saw the mistake of manifesting it, and this gave me the reputation of being one of the most modest of the young writers; which reminds me of an old axiom: "Assume a virtue that you have not got, and after many days you will really have it." Or perhaps you will only appear to have it.

But all this time I was growing in the power to think, and I was beginning to think on new lines. In consequence of being on a reform paper it was my duty to keep track of the labor movement as it was then developing in San Francisco. I attended the meetings of the various labor factions quite freely, and was often called on for a speech, but had not the courage to attempt it.

When I first began to go to these meetings I had great sympathy for the laborers; but on close acquaintance with them I lost it. I soon saw that not more than one in a hundred had any higher ambition than to change places with his employer, so that he might have it in his power to live without work. The exceptional one in a hundred, by virtue of superior intelligence, soon raised himself to a better position where he became satisfied that the law of evolution was able to express itself in him without any more fuss on his part.

It was here that I began to see the might of individuality. I soon knew that individualization was salvation, and that every effort short of it could only be palliative. Men must be men before they could earn the reward of manhood.

It is very true that the capitalists against whom the efforts of the laborers were arrayed, were no more men in the true sense than the laborers were. I saw that their accumulations were mere fortuitious aggregations on the animal plane; but this fact did not invalidate my position so far as the laborer was concerned. He was not any more of a man because his employer fell short of the mark. In fact, I found that there was very little manhood to be discovered in the entire pot of mush; and from writing sympathetically and generously about them as I had formerly done, I began to score them with burning words and a pen that quivered with indignation.

To think that they should be content to meet at stated periods for the simple purpose of airing their grievances, and abusing the men for whom they were working, began to look like a confession of weakness to me. "Either do something or shut up," I used to say when they approached me individually. "I am tired of your make believe in courage and manhood. There is not a man among you, and you know it; or you would know it if you knew what it required to constitute a man."

In the meantime, however, my articles began to attract some attention outside of San Francisco, and I had an offer from the *Chicago Express*, then the leading paper in the world in the reform movement, to go on its editorial staff.

Ada was just married, and Florence would soon be; and I accepted the offer.

But even when I went to Chicago I was almost ready for emancipation from the movement I was writing for; and it was only a little over a year until I gave it my parting thrust in the following article:

SLAVES AND MASTERS.

I know the slave-driver and I know the slave, and I say that the slave-driver, selfish as he is, is a gentleman in comparison with the slave. There is nothing in all the world so ignoble as a slave. He is in his true position so long as he willingly bears his servitude. He is fit for nothing else. Why should I care that his back is bent with the burdens of another? Why should I be distressed at his wrongs? His wrongs are his rights so long as he bears them willingly. That which would be the wrongs of freemen are for him his just deserts.

I mean to speak the truth from this time on. I have coddled the slave and called him a man, when I knew there was no manhood in him. I will do it no longer. On the contrary, I mean to assert everywhere and on all occasions that he who wears a fetter needs it; that he who bears a kick, deserves it. I wash my hands of spirits so slavish as to take part in the injustice that is crushing them. Moreover, I say that the bent back of the laborer, the horny hands, the coarse, distorted features, and the general ugliness that marks him, are a confession of his own sins in abetting the sins of his master.

I desire to speak face to face to you, the slaves of

the nineteenth century; to tell you how I have seen every effort made by philanthropists for your benefit fall to the ground worthless, because your own base influence was against it. There are labor papers working for you to which you have never contributed the cost of a drink of whisky. I have seen more and worse than this; that you have no respect for any man but the one that kicks you; and no trust in any power but that which crushes you.

You are the obstacle, the only obstacle, in the way of race emancipation. Your masters are a handful; you are legion. Your masters are intelligent, and though they will not voluntarily relax their selfish grip on the good things of this world, not one of them would dare refuse if you stood up for your rights. But you are more besotted with the far-off dazzle of their gold than they are with its possession. They have moments when they reflect how their money has been gathered at your expense; moments when they almost wish that the system that fosters robbery, that makes gold king, that puts in abeyance every noble impulse, could be changed. But you adore the system; you doff the ragged cap and bend the servile knee before the baser part of these men's natures, and your only desire for liberty is for the sake of emulating their vices instead of their virtues. They know this, and they know that a social rupture that would transform you into millionaires at their expense would be the greatest possible calamity.

For these men, selfish as they are, have benefited the race through the thrift of enterprise. They have built railroads and made the different races of men as one nation. They have utilized your dumb energies to serve mankind in serving themselves. They have used you as machines, running your services at the lowest cost compatible with your lives, until at last they begin to supplant you with cheaper wood and iron. And all this because they could do it; because you permitted it.

They have done right. You were and are as worthless as the dirt under your feet, except for the power of physical contraction and expansion in your muscles. You will not think. The moment one of you begins to think he ceases to belong to that class to whom this article is addressed. Your faces are prone to the ground to which your worn-out bodies are rapidly hastening. You plod and delve from day to day, never casting admiring eyes aloft, except when your masters with liveried attendants splash mud over you from their carriage wheels as they pass in haughty splendor.

And you have the privileges of citizenship in a land where such privilege is denied by you to those whose intelligence ten generations of culture will scarcely enable you to comprehend—the intelligent women of these States. And what is more, being in the majority, you hold this magnificent element in check, and prevent its pure current and turn it away from that point where it would be of incalculable benefit, and where above all other influences it would benefit you and lift you out of your down-trodden condition. For American women above all others are your sympathizers. They resent for you the wrongs your craven souls accept. And you turn up your noses contemptuously when reference is made to their political equality.

What are you going to do? Your muscles, the only part of you your masters ever needed, have been supplanted by the more economical substitution of machinery. Are you willing to cumber the earth as useless lumber, or are you willing to come up to the dignity of manhood by an effort to comprehend the true situation and to arouse within your brains the thought that will meet it? There are only two ways for you. Your muscles are superseded. The demand for them becomes continually more limited. The

world calls on all men now for brain. It asks you for
thought, that through thought it may develop the
finer and as yet unexplored forces of nature. If you
refuse to respond to this call, there remains the other
alternative—to die and give place to those who are
susceptible to the higher impulses of a more refined
age.—*Chicago Express.*

This article to a superficial thinker seems hard and
cruel; but it is neither. It is simple truth. The
slaves of labor are where they are because they will
not use their brains. *Thought* has power to redeem
them by showing them a true estimate of their own
worth. But so long as they will not think they are
not men. They are on a lower plane than that of
men, and they are receiving treatment in conformity
with the plane they are on. They have only their
own ignorance to blame, and this is what they never
think of blaming.

Intelligence is the lifting power. Intelligence in-
dividualizes. No man can seek a knowledge of himself introspectively without discovering the rudiments
of godhood within him. It is this discovery which
gradually lifts him in the scale of being to a place
where he looks with level eyes into the face of all
other men. When he is able to do this his fetters—

no matter what they have been—actually fall. Better positions in business open up to him; better surroundings come about him in answer to his increased consciousness of power. Let a man once proclaim himself a freeman from this high point of intellectual seeing, and all the world hastens to respond.

CHAPTER XVIII.

A GLIMPSE OF THE PROMISED LAND.

In finishing the previous chapter, I jumped an interval of at least two years, and perhaps more; and I must retrace my steps in order to give my readers a true idea of how my growing thought was pushing me on, and away from the pessimistic beliefs that had led me into the kicking field of reform.

In first looking abroad over the world, and seeing the inequality of position among the masses, we naturally resent it, and begin to search for some person or persons to whom we lay the blame. In California where the capitalist flourished in extraordinary glory, and where his tyranny was more felt than in other states, owing to the fact that the mass of the laborers there were the sons of the bravest men that the republic has produced, namely, the pioneers who cut their way through such enormous obstacles to reach the state in 1849, there was the loudest possible call for sympathy and assistance from one so situated as I had been.

I wanted somebody to blame for the situation; somebody besides the laborers themselves, and I became a very acceptable writer on an antagonistic plane of effort.

I believed that certain social and political reform was all that was necessary to enable men and women to rise in the scale of being, to much higher positions of thought and action than have ever yet been attained. And so I worked for the accomplishment of this end. That is, I did my little best for it. I was an unknown writer, and my influence was small; but I was in earnest and put my whole soul in my work, believing in it with great fervency.

But at every step I was disappointed. The people themselves for whom I was laboring were the greatest disappointment of all. They were dead to any sense of power within themselves, and were only alive to what they considered their wrongs. No thoughts of a higher intellectual growth stimulated them in their effort to obtain greater financial independence. Their ideas of liberty—if gratified—would lead in the direction of unbridled license. They knew nothing of freedom in the true sense of the word. They had no idea that their fetters were of their making, no less than their masters, and were all to be resolved into one short sentence—complete ignorance of their own undeveloped possibilities. They cared nothing for these possibilities. They would not institute within themselves the search for what they needed in order to secure liberty. They did not know, and did not seem to wish to know, that each man holds his own heaven in his personality, and that the careful unfolding of that personality will yield him *all there is.* They preferred the clashing of opinions that were not based upon the foundation where individual growth begins, but instead were the mixed outcome of life's mistaken beliefs.

Instead of growing nearer to these people in sympathy, I was growing away from them. At first I did not see the drift of this thing, and made many futile attempts to regain my interest. I got so I hated to write a reform article, and as to reading one from any of the numerous exchanges, I simply could not do it.

It would be difficult for me to describe the confusion of mind I was in. My duties in the office of the *Chicago Express*—though very light—became a nightmare. Major Smith, the owner of the paper, was generosity itself. He was, and is, one of the noblest men I have ever met; my fast friend then and now; and if every soul on earth should prove a disappointment, the remembrance of him, his splendid manhood, his loyalty to his highest convictions of truth, and, indeed, his whole mentality would always stand before me in justification of my unshaken faith in the godhood of man.

I am conscious now that Major Smith himself was also losing interest in the people for whom he was laboring so faithfully; but at the time I went off the paper, he did not know it. He was still putting every effort of his strong, great life into his work, regardless of the fact that those for whom he thought and labored and sacrificed were so irresponsive and unthankful. He went out of the paper later, and has since applied his fine business ability to building up another enterprise, which has been wonderfully successful.

But when I left the *Express* he was displeased. He had the right to think me ungrateful. My action must have looked so to him. But I could not remain in the work. It is true that I was then incapable of analyzing the impulse which prompted me so powerfully to abandon it forever. I only recognized the impulse, and I was obedient to it.

I had come to feel my work degrading to the higher possibilities of my brain, although I was unable to get

even a glimpse of what those possibilities might be.
I have been almost recklessly obedient to that something which constantly goes before us, alluring us
onward. I have said a thousand times that my lack
of success lay in the fact of my incapability to be true
to any idea or any line of thought or action long
enough to carry it to completion. I did not know that
this was mental growth, and so deplored it as being
the one element in my character that prevented me
from making a success of anything I attempted.

To illustrate. The morning came, when, after dragging myself to the *Express* office, I sat at my desk
gloomy and despondent. I went presently to the
Major's desk, and told him I wished to start a paper of
my own. He let me know that the sea of journalism
was very tempestuous, and many barks were wrecked
in it; and of the few that succeeded only a very small
number were real successes. He begged me, for my
own interest, to remain where I was. When he saw
that his argument failed to shake me, he turned back
to his desk very gravely, and I felt that if I left his
employment under the circumstances I would lose the
best friend I had in the world.

On the road of progress it often happens that the
warmest friendship may become a tyranny that has to

be broken. Nothing should hold the outward-bound soul, and nothing could hold me. I would be free.

What a compelling force the ideal is! And yet on that November morning I had no glimpse of the ideal that usually presented so many allurements for attracting me from sober duty. It was simply the fact that I had reached the end of another experience, and must quit, and prospect for the beginning of the line of travel that did, undoubtedly, unite with it, and that I was willing to trust blindly in an effort to find.

I sat at my desk deliberately reasoning out the situation. Major Smith had spoken of my bread and butter as being involved in my new effort. I thought about this, and anathematized the suggestion. "What do I care for bread and butter unless it feeds me to the actualization of higher and better hopes?" I said. "I don't want bread and butter except on my own terms. I don't want life on its present inharmonious plane. If there is to be nothing better in it than I have seen and felt, then it may close to-day for all I care."

As I write these words I go back to that time; and I still believe the logic I then used to be one of the truest bits of wisdom that a growing soul can adopt. I did really lose all fear of want as completely as if entirely emancipated from every need of our present lives. I got up and put on my cloak and hood and went down into the street. The morning had been sunshiny, but cold, when I came. It was now gloomed over despairingly. I never saw a more dismal sky. The sleet, borne on a strong wind, struck me in the face; the sidewalks were coated with ice. As I stood at the foot of the stairs I opened my purse. I had only twenty-five cents between me and starvation. I had not a friend in the city but the one I had just left. I was my own sole dependence. There was no prop in the world on which I could lean, and I knew it with the most vivid sense of realization. More than this, I knew that there was no one I wanted to lean upon. I doubt whether in the history of the race there has been a soul who stood more erect in a position of such complete isolation. I was so far removed from fear and anxiety that I gloried in my aloneness. I walked those icy streets like a school boy just freed from restraint. My years fell from me as completely as if death had turned my spirit loose in Paradise.

Back to my boarding house to face the scowls of my landlord, whose prudent eye questioned my untimely return, and who shrewdly and rightly suspected that next week's board bill would go unpaid. Then to my room and to pen and paper. I was fired by my sense of freedom; and what I wrote must have found an echo in hundreds of imprisoned spirits; for that article made my paper a success.

Late in the afternoon my landlord came to my room, embarrassed, but resolute. He wanted to know how matters stood.

"Have you been discharged by the chief?"

"No, I discharged myself. I am not going to be anybody's hired man any longer."

"Is your bread insured?"

"I don't concede your right to question me, but I believe I am glad you take the liberty. My bread is insured."

"How?"

"I am going to start a paper of my own, and I am going to make it a success. Sit down while I read you the first article I have written for it."

He did so, and I read the article. The subject was "I."

It was a wonderful article. I am sure of this from the effect it produced—not only on my landlord—but on others. It was a declaration of individuality; it would have been a protest against bonds, but for the fact that it sounded notes of freedom far above all thought of bonds, and clear out of sight of them. It had wings to it; it arose aloft; it lifted those who read it into the air with it.

That it had this effect on me was not surprising: but when I saw its effect on my landlord I was amazed. His face, which was naturally sodden, had become illuminated. After a pause he said, "I have perfect confidence in your ability to succeed. In fact I am ready to gamble on you. I have twenty thousand dollars in bank, and you can draw on me for all you need."

Then I confessed that I was without means; but I refused to take his money, only asking him to wait a few weeks on my board bill.

From that time on, no queen could have been treated with more courtesy. One day in my absence he moved my things down from my single room on the third floor to a lovely suite of three rooms on the parlor floor. Again and again he offered me money, which I steadily refused.

Fate was working rapidly in my favor at that time. Evidently the state of mental freedom I had achieved was putting a compulsion on externals in a very peremptory way. And oh! how happy I was. I drew the design for the heading of my paper, and was so pleased with it that several times I got up in the night to look at it. I took it to the lithographer and had a plate made. It was sent to me by a boy several days later without the bill.

When my writing was quite finished I went to the largest publishing house in the city and ordered twenty thousand copies of the paper, to be delivered at my rooms on a certain day.

In the meantime I was addressing wrappers as fast as I could, and making other preparations for mailing sample copies.

On the third day after they were mailed I got $11.00 on subscription. This was wealth. The next day brought more. Not long afterwards a rich man in Boston sent me a check for $250.00. Another sent $25.00, and others from $5.00 to $10.00. It was the clarion tones of that article on the "I," that caught the public. I wish I had the article now; but I have lost it. I have written several articles since then on the same subject, but the pure bell metal was lacking in the tone of all of them. Not one produced the effect that the first one did.

It was the mood I was in that made the first one what it was. I was free; for the time being I had achieved an extraordinary height in human experience, and I wrote from that height. I was absolutely fearless. The thought of poverty or any coming trouble could not daunt me. Every form of anxiety was beneath me. The doubts of my own ability to succeed, which had always haunted my mind, were entirely gone. Heavens, what an attitude it was!

If I could have remained there, who knows what might have happened? I believe this is what Jesus meant when he said, "If I be lifted up from the earth, I will draw all men unto me."

To be lifted is simply to be freed from the doubts and fears born of the world's ignorant beliefs with regard to man's capacity. Being freed from doubts and fears for a time, I was lifted.

It is true that I tumbled down to the race level again, but the experience has been worth more than a hundred ordinary lives to me. It taught me a mighty lesson. If I could reach that position once, even for an hour, then it was possible for me to reach it and remain in it forever. And if possible for me, then it was possible for all. There must be some basis of brain force—though scarcely developed in any one—from which such thoughts as I had could be projected. It was unreasonable not to see this; and to-day it is my hope and the hope of the world that such basis does exist in the human organism, and that time, introspection and patient effort will develop it.

And if developed, what then? This question did not face me for immediate solution. It was a question that shaped itself in the years that followed. Neither did it actually begin with the experience I have recorded. There were years of close observation and earnest, though broken and disjointed thought that led up to it.

I wonder now how far back it was when I conceived the idea that man had it in him to conquer all things, even death? It must have been born with me. It made me a physical coward and a mental hero. This seemed a great misfortune for a long time. But now when life is passing completely from a belief in the physical to a belief in the mental, it will be a misfortune no longer.

For years after I left the church I kept reading the Bible, with the belief that I could find a new meaning to it. I went through it again and, again. At last I thought I saw that it held the concentrated hopes of many ages, all pointing to the time when man should overcome death. And I concluded that this was why it was preserved as holy writ. It was the vital spark of a hundred dead generations, going forward to reincarnation in a superior race not yet born; a race that would be able to overcome. Oh! how the thought took hold on me.

I saw no way to its fulfillment, and yet I was disposed to experiment with it in various ways. My vivid imagination elaborated many a scheme pointing towards it, each of which faded, to be replaced by others. And so the time passed and nothing seemed to be done.

Then came the memorable period when I stood alone for a few days in the splendor of individuality, and saw, as in some powerful telescope, the mighty possibilities of man; and I knew that he had no impediment in his progress but himself; no jungle he could not penetrate but the jungle of his own doubts and fears; no load he could not carry but that of his own self-constructed anxieties.

CHAPTER XIX.

ALL IS MIND: THE SUBSTANCE OF WHICH WORLDS ARE MADE IS MENTAL SUBSTANCE: THOUGHT HAS BUILT THE VISIBLE UNIVERSE.

Whether it would be better through the remaining chapters of "A Search For Freedom" to confine myself to the thought development, which has established me so firmly in a belief of the possibility of conquering all appearances of evil, even those intensely obdurate ones we call old age and death, or whether it would be more satisfactory to my readers for me to tell of my external life and its conquests—for it has been very full of them—I am at a loss to decide. At all events, I shall now give a chapter from the unseen side; and let the farther narration of events rest with my future feelings about it.

As I gathered mental power from the exercise of my reasoning faculties, it became more and more apparent to me that these faculties were limitless, and that their unrestrained growth through future ages would enable us to conquer every obstacle that might oppose us; that we were virtually masters of life and death by reason of the unlimited power of unfoldment within our own brains.

In all my speculations I clung to the Bible. My brain was so fertile in theories that the very number of them confused me. I felt that I needed ballast; and as the Bible had previously been my last resort in every emergency, it became so again.

True, there was a time, just after my leaving the church, that I was afraid of the Bible, and turned almost violent in my attitude toward it. I accused it of being my jailer, and trembled lest it take me once more into captivity. But I got over this feeling and made friends with it. I began to put my own construction upon it, and a most astonishing construction it was. It was the book of life, I thought, not because a God above and beyond our power to comprehend had written it, but because it reflected the ideal faculties of so many of the sun-tipped brains of the race.

The magnificent ideality in the prophets and seers, whose hopes have been projected in the book, pointed to a time when man should be big enough intellectually to conquer all the seemingly opposing forces in life, and proclaim himself master of death.

Having formed this belief, I then went to work to find in the Bible the evidence necessary to establish it more firmly.

And it is astonishing how much of such evidence I really found there. The new construction I put upon almost every chapter would make a book of great interest, as a matter of curiosity, whether it would possess any actual merit or not. But to this day it seems to me that from the centre of self in each individual who wrote the Bible, there went out a stream of light leading far into the future, and partly illuminating the time when man would be a free citizen of this world, with power to construct a most potent heaven out of it. The prophecies relate to this life; they concern bodies, and not souls; they deal with this world, and not some future one.

Much of the Bible contains wonderful truth of a purely metaphysical character. Many of its narratives are delineations of truths inherent in the human constitution, and relating to certain phases of conscientious individual development.

Who, for instance, has not been in the whale's belly, imprisoned there for the same reason that Jonah was; that is, because he was afraid to express his highest conviction?

God (the voice of his highest conviction) told Jonah to go to Nineveh and proclaim, "Yet forty days and Nineveh shall be destroyed!" Jonah refused to do it. He was afraid to trust the word, though spoken from the highest point of intelligence he knew. Then his whole mentality went into darkness, and he could see no light anywhere. He was dead within himself; he was shirking his duty; he was "denying his God." All nature seemed arrayed against him; no new, vitalizing thought was born in his brain, and could not be so long as the pressure of an undone deed was pushing against his conscience for execution.

The entire meaning of the little narrative is this: Belief becomes potent only in externalization. When we refuse to express or to externalize our most peremptory thoughts, they trouble us to such an extent that growth is stultified so long as this condition remains. It was fear that held Jonah from expressing his positive belief. His case is worthy of record. There is no instance of courageous mastery in history that excels it. He did what he was afraid to do because he thought he was right.

And in the end Neneveh was not destroyed. There can never be a grander lesson taught than this last fact. The word he had spoken in utmost faith did not prove true. And what does this mean? It means that on the road of progression a man must do and be the best he knows regardless of consequences, regardless of the fact that to-morrow's knowledge may prove every assertion of to-day an error. This is forging ahead in spite of opposition, the opposition of ignorance, which is the only opposition any one ever has. And this forging ahead, cleaving a way through the untried jungle of doubts and fears that surrounds us, is growth.

The story of Jonah is the story of a man who dared to stand by his convictions in the face of his own fears.

The Bible is full of such records if properly understood. All of them relate to the building of man—the master.

The Bible had again become my guide in my effort to see my way out of the clouds and shadows, that pressed so densely upon my mental vision, while I was attempting to find the road leading away from disease, old age and death.

The love of beauty has amounted almost to a mania with me all my life. I doubt whether I ever was inspired to an effort of any kind, that the hope of making something appear more attractive did not actuate me.

And what inducements life was holding out! How things did grow, and kept growing! The mystery of perpetual unfoldment was in everything. I did not reason on this wonderful fact at the time of which I am writing, but I had an undefined perception of it that was all pervading, and that filled me with a sense of security. The words that most frequently came to me were, "I don't understand now, but I shall do so sometime; I can wait."

The fact is, I was growing almost as unconsciously as the peach grows, simply because I was non-resistant to the ubiquitous good that surely does pervade all things. I had turned my mind loose from dogmas of every description, and the *eternal life* was beginning to flow through it.

I talked to some of my friends on the subject of conquering death, but no one took any interest. Many of them said that death itself was a conquest that liberated the spirit from this gross body; and that was what they desired.

But I knew better than this. I knew that the approach to death was by the road of many and constantly increasing weaknesses, and that death was the culmination of all weakness. There was no semblance of conquest in it; nothing but defeat. It was the overcoming of the will. People do not want to die; and to be compelled to do what one does not want to do is surrendery, and not mastery.

I suppose I was gradually growing stronger in my selfhood, for I was beginning to lay claims to life in a way that set aside all limitations. There was a growing strength within me that caused me to repudiate every form of fatalism. The preacher might preach of death; a voice within me negatived his word. Everything in the world, and that had ever been in it, denied my claim, but I only made it stronger in the face of such opposition.

"*I am*," was my constant thought; and these words always bristled with a sense of unconquerableness.

I can trace the growth of my will step by step from the moment that I recorded in my own mind my claim to deathlessness.

It became a difficult thing for me to stick to my text so far as my paper, *The Woman's World*, was concerned. It was a woman's suffrage paper, and I had lost interest in the subject, in view of the greater subject that really does circumference all reforms.

Mary Eddy, the author of "Science and Health," got hold of a copy of *The Woman's World*, and wrote me that I was almost a Christian Scientist. With her letter came her book. It was then in two small volumes. I tried to read it; but it was nonsense to me. Some of her later editions make her meaning clearer, but the one she sent me did not contain a single thought that was in any manner related to my way of thinking.

With the books and the letter came an advertisement of her and her work she wished me to insert in payment of the books. The advertisement was long enough to occupy the most of the space in my little paper. I threw the whole outfit in the waste basket, and forgot about it until she wrote again ordering me most peremptorily to send the books back. The books had been in use until they were nearly worn out before they reached me, and the curious part was that any person could ever have read them enough to even soil them.

This was the first I had heard of Christian Science. It made no impression on me. Later I had my interest aroused, and joined a class in Chicago, where I think I came into a clear understanding of the whole movement.

I soon learned that the movement had no objective point; it was the brewing of an idea that did not understand its own meaning; it was the undeveloped soul of a new truth not yet clothed with the body that would make it of practical benefit to the world. It was a prophecy of mighty things to come, and this was all it was, or is. But that of which it was the nebular and prophetic beginning was on its way to the rescue of mankind, and it is growing in power every day. Christian Science is the outer vestibule leading to a mighty system of thought. Entering into it is the beginning of salvation from sorrow and disease, old age and death. Remaining in it, under the mistaken belief that it is all there is, will not permanently save any person. Salvation depends upon eternal progression; eternal growth in the knowledge of life. No one can stand still, and yet continue to live. Death is the penalty of stagnation. Indeed, death and stagnation are synonymous terms.

This is what ails the churches. They do not save; they only postpone. The time to save is when salvation is most needed; the place to save is where life's ills are thickest. And where is that? Right here in the world to-day.

And what are life's ills? They are sickness and sorrow and poverty and old age and death. These are the things we wish to be saved from; and now is a better time to begin the work of salvation than after death.

For who knows what the words "after death" may mean? Endless numbers of people think they know; and theories concerning this state lie thick all down the ages, but not one item of absolute knowledge has been brought forth.

Nature is the most potent truth we have. Looking within these natural selves of ours, we find that the strongest of all implanted desires is for life, and more life, and still more life; life at first trying to reach out beyond the grave; and then—when all its springs have been strengthened by its constantly growing hope and faith, comes the more vital thought of life that need not yield to death; life that bridges the grave with intelligence—the knowing how to continue to live.

Gradually the great truth dawns that man is master of himself and his surroundings; that there is no power in the universe that prescribes his limitations; that says to him, "Stay where you are; go no farther."

And so, by slow degrees, I came to recognize man's place in the world, and his relation to his surroundings; and great joy—even exultation—took possession of me. Time, fate, circumstance, were no longer my foes nor even my obstructions.

Before I reached this condition, I had—through

years of concentrated thought—climbed to the light of the one truth on which salvation from old age and death rests.

It is the mighty fact that all is mind; that the substance which in the past we have called dead matter *is a mental substance;* a substance, every atom of which, thinks, or holds in latency the power to think. This one truth when understood is itself sole conqueror of old age and death. Nothing more is needed but the perfect understanding of it to close every avenue of weakness to every member of the race, and to start all persons on an unbroken road of endless progression through the coming centuries; and to start them, too, in a way that insures greater strength to them with every advance step they take.

If a man is a purely mental creature, and this is precisely what he is, then *knowing is being.* The less he knows, the weaker he is and the more liable to be overcome by the obstructions he meets, and the more surely will he fall a victim to disease and death. Whereas, the more he knows, the stronger he becomes and the easier he finds it to overcome difficulties, until a perception of the fact that he is master of all things begins to dawn on him. A mental perception of individual strength is invariably a physical perception of it also, because mind and body are one. In other words, the body is all mind, of which thought—the positive pole of the body—is the shaping and directing power.

As I have said previously, the grandest truth of this or any age is the fact that man is a mental statement of knowledge, and not a physical creation of decaying matter.

This is true not only of man but of all things that exist; it is true of the grass and of the birds and bees; it is true of the rocks; it is the ample explanation of geology; it is true of the stars; it is the basis of astronomy, and accounts for the formation of planets and for their movement in their spheres. It explains all things; it is the key that unlocks the entire mystery of life and death and disease and of every enigma that has ever presented itself for solution to man, or that ever will present itself.

The knowledge that all is mind, that the universe in all its parts from atoms to suns is but a mental statement, will—when studied out—prove its own explanation, and establish the fact that there is nothing concealed from the growing mind of man.

Moreover, this statement—that all is mind—is the great turning point in the race's history. It is the point of ascension from the fatalistic theory of cause and effect, as based upon a belief in dead matter, to the freedom of personal creativeness, through the acquisition of such truths as go with the understanding that man is a mental creature who has ever been the accretion of thought; and who can go on in an unbroken line of growth by continuing to think newer and nobler and higher thoughts than he has heretofore been thinking.

The objection brought to bear on this idea comes from persons who will not use their reasoning powers enough to see the matter in its entirety. They say, "Why, mind is an invisible thing; and if man is all mind, then he could not be seen," etc.

But mind is not invisible. Everything of which we receive knowledge through any one of the senses is mind—the trees, the rocks, the water, all things. And what proof have we that they are mind? This; each one of them is a certain form of knowing. Each one of them is a recognition of life. To recognize is to think. The atom thinks; it recognizes within itself the law of attraction, and in obedience to this recognition it unites with some other atom, thus becoming the commencement of a more complex life than it had heretofore been.

But this subject has been so thoroughly explained in my other works, that I must pass on and leave it alone. That it is worth investigating the reader may well believe, when I say that it lies at the foundation of man's power to become master of life and all of life's forces, even to the overcoming of his last enemy—death.

The mighty facts springing from a knowledge of the true solution of man—namely—that he is a mental creature, self-created and self-creating, through his power to evolve knowledge out of his own organism, has been going on for years in my mind; and converts to the idea have been quite rapidly made.

And this decides me to go back and bring up some personal experiences, that I had thought I could complete this "Search For Freedom" without touching upon.

That I have found freedom can be seen by any one who has read the latter part of this work carefully. I am, indeed, emancipated from every form of anxiety and fear, and this is freedom. I have become emancipated through the knowledge of man's powers of mastery; and I know that the exercise of such powers by him is demonstration over everything that has ever seemed to hold him in bondage.

CHAPTER XX.

COMING TO FLORIDA.

The trouble with an ordinary autobiography is that one does not know when to stop it. The author is rarely so accommodating as to die and leave the last chapter to be finished by an addenda from the publisher.

And if this is the case with the autobiography of one who believes in the power of death, and who expects to die, how much more difficult it is where the author is quite sure she is in process of overcoming death, and who could make a new chapter to her book every week through eternity.

This is precisely my case. The increasing vitality of my thought since I began to find out that man is not the creature of blind fate, neither the puppet of a God outside of himself, has added so much to my bodily powers—the body and thought being one—that I really cannot, in looking forward, see anything for myself but a still greater increase of life's forces and, therefore, still greater length of days, all pointing to the overcoming of old age and death.

Once, while pondering deeply upon this subject—
this was before I came into an understanding of the
law of growth—I had what a superstitious person
might call a vision. I seemed to lapse from my state
of consciousness for a time, and to find myself far
away from my surroundings. I was with my living
children walking on the seashore. It was high tide,
the beach was narrow, and the waves were coming in
and wetting our feet and our skirts, impeding our
progress and making us quite wretched.

The sand dunes rose high on the left hand as we
moved along laboriously. On top of the sand dunes,
keeping pace with us as we went onward, was Jennie—
the little girl I had lost. It was high and dry where
she was; and I watched her light and graceful movements eagerly, with my face turned up toward her so
constantly I scarcely noted the wretchedness of my
own condition. After going on in this way for some
time, our path turned gradually upward, while the
path Jennie was on began to turn downward.
Presently it terminated in a lovely little valley about
half way up to the top of the dunes. It was the
quaintest little valley imaginable. It gave me the
feeling of having been translated out of some old
Bible story. In the midst of it was a well walled

about with stone, and over the well an arch with the words, "This is the water of life. He that drinketh of this water shall thirst no more." The water was of diamond clearness, and we drank it and felt rested. Then we sat down on the stone seat, and who should be with us there but Jennie? And oh! the shining light in her eyes, and oh! the happiness, the sense of completeness that fell upon us, never—as it seemed—to be broken any more!

This circumstance made a strong impression on me at the time. It gave me courage to hold to my highest thoughts and hopes. And yet I should have held to them anyhow. I could not drop them; they held to me; they were a part of me.

In the meantime, while I was nourishing the thoughts that pointed so constantly to man's conquest of death, and to his ability to work this planet over in conformity with the high ideals which I knew he possessed in latency, and while I had hard work to keep from boring my friends with superfluous talk on the subject, I met Mr. C. C. Post, on whom I made such an impression with my earnestness that he encouraged me to tell him all about it. What he really thought of me in the early days of our acquaintance I do not know; but if he got tired of me at times, he got rested and came back to see me again. In July, 1883, I was married to him; and I believe I can truthfully say that our relations have been a source of the greatest pleasure and growth to each. Personally he is pleasing in manner and appearance, with the face of a student and the temperament of an artist, all flavored with a sense of humor that adds greatly to his power to please. A man of broad thought and ready speech, a poet as well as a logical reasoner, he is widely known as a writer and speaker upon both political and metaphysical subjects. His articles in *Freedom* have attracted more universal attention and favorable comment than have those of any other correspondent, just as his published works of fiction outsold all other works of their class at the time they were issued; and they still continue to sell. My regret is that his time is so consumed in business affairs connected with the upbuilding of the place, and the hote for which he feels himself responsible, and, indeed, for the development of all our plans for the future, as to prevent him from giving his entire attention to writing and the study of metaphysical subjects.

But who knows what man's relation to woman is? It may be that his executive power bears a strictly

counterpartal relation to her ideality. One thing
certain, woman is not "lesser man," as Tennyson said;
she is all that man is not. They are to each other
complement, fulfillment. But this is a matter not to
be discussed now—at a time when woman is only
beginning to be faintly awakened to what she is, and
when man knows no more about her than she knows
about herself.

Some three years after my marriage to Mr. Post we
came South. We were on a search for conditions.
We hardly knew what the conditions would be; but
we had worn out the old ones, and had been worn out
in them, until a complete change became imperative.

Indeed, Mr. Post was a very sick man. He had
worked too hard at the desk, and death threatened him
in the shape of consumption. When we left Chicago
not one of our friends expected to see him alive
again.

This was soon after we had begun to make a study
of metaphysical subjects, and the opportunity of test-
ing what little we knew about the power of mind to
control matter, was surely present in his case.

We went to Douglasville, Georgia, and there, in a
little country hotel, we fought the battle with death
and won the victory. As health began to be es-

tablished in Mr. Post's wasted frame, a wild curiosity was manifested to find out what cured him. It was believed that I possessed some secret power that was denied to others, and I became a marked individual in the community. Especially the negroes were affected by Mr. Post's cure, and they came to me with their complaints and begged to be cured also. At this point I could have done the work that Schlatter did and established a world-wide reputation as a healer; for among an intensely negative people, it is only necessary to speak the word for health and it will soon manifest itself.

At first it was the colored people who came to me for relief; but soon there was another class came. Southern society is divided into three classes; the negroes, the poorer class of white people who are tenants on the land they plant, and the upper class who are property owners, and in every way superior to the others. I only had a short experience with the middle class when the more intelligent and refined people began to crowd all the others out.

I soon got tired of the whole matter, especially as it took up my entire time and there was no money of any consequence in it; and we needed money. I had sold *The Woman's World* before leaving Chicago, and

Mr. Post had been unable for months to earn anything with his pen. It was quite a long time before he recovered his mental vigor sufficiently to enter the field of literature again.

And even when he became stronger his inclinations turned against it; he wished for some ground in which to dig and plant. He had been brought up on a farm, and it was strange to see how he really longed to come into close relations with old mother earth once more.

The result was that we bought some land adjoining the town, and began to improve it. But money was none too plenty, and neither of us was earning anything.

But all the time, every day and hour, my thoughts kept running more and more on the subject of how to overcome disease, old age and death. My experience in healing the people about me threw wonderful light over the whole field of man's, as yet, undeveloped power in this direction. I saw how rapidly all negative beliefs—which are beliefs grounded in ignorance of the law of evolution—were displaced and wiped out by the positive beliefs generated in a brain that refused to accept any statement of man's limitation.

Each day my former belief in an overruling power with its fatalistic results was drawing down from the mirage of an imaginary heaven and coming closer to the earth. This forced me into the study of nature and her laws; and I studied them so faithfully that they brought me splendid reward. I became a veritable product of earth, submerged in her fruitful soil—so to speak—where, like some seed or bulb, I took root and began to feel the throbbing pulse of mother earth quickening the life within me.

I voluntarily became as a little child. I presented no opposing belief to the influx of natural knowledge which is constantly flowing from the earth in expressions of use and beauty, and which still holds life for us in greater quantity than man dreams of, if we will but discard visionary theories that lead us far away from the nourishing breast of this dear mother into regions of thin vapor where we starve.

That man's course is upward, and that he will eventually *grow* away from the earth is true; but the effort to lift him above the earth before the earth has matured him—that is, before she has vested her entire power of reproduction in him, is like taking a young plant out of the ground and suspending it in the air and then expecting it to grow.

The man's hopes and beliefs have been lifted above the present plane of his living. He believes himself to be the result of some supernatural creation, and dependent on some supernatural power; when in strict truth he is but a vegetable evolved into higher knowledge of the law of growth than the other vegetables that go to sustain his life. The same forces contribute to his existence that contribute to the existence of a cabbage or a cow. The man is both cabbage and cow, with the added intelligence of centuries of unfoldment by the acquisition of more experiences than the cabbage and cow have had, which experiences have given him a superior intelligence to that of his progenitors, and, by reason of his superior intelligence, a superior form.

For intelligence expresses itself in form. From beginning to end—if there could be an end—in every form, and under all circumstances, it holds true that *knowing is being.* And this is because the universe is not composed of dead matter, but of the vital, ever changing, ever substantial and real manifestation of *mind.*

Mind is intelligence in manifestation; it is thought in expression. To say that a man is as he believes, is the key that unlocks the whole situation. Everything from the grain of sand up through each ascending group or species in the scale of existence is just what it believes. This means that its form and its powers are but the expression of as much as it knows.

The one great truth standing head and shoulders above all the truths ever ripened by the human brain is the truth that all is mind or intelligence. The universe is but a huge system of brain, evolving thoughts; and thoughts are things. They are actual substances. They may be thoughts rooted in the ground as the trees, or they may be thoughts flying in the air as the birds, but in every case they are thoughts—generating still other thoughts.

That life is perpetuated by the growth and development of thought from within these human bodies of ours is a scientific fact. It does not rest on hearsay, nor is it an idle theory like the baseless fabric of salvation by the grace of God. It is a demonstrable thing when the foundation principle underlying all truth is found. And the foundation principle is at last found in the statement that the substance commonly accepted as dead matter is living, vital mind, expressing itself in the myriad of forms everywhere to be seen and felt and heard.

Man's continued powers of growth rest on the fact that thought is life, and that his ability to project thought into higher channels than has ever been done before is his positive guarantee of more life, and life on a higher or more positive plane than he has heretofore known.

More thought, higher thought is more life and higher life; and both are vital force. An acceleration of vital force expressed in our bodies means the banishment of disease, old age and death.

As I said before, this thing is susceptible of the most scientific explanation. It is a fact, and is being demonstrated satisfactorily by more than one person now living.

I can look back in my own experience and see the gradual ripening of thought up to the point where I knew for a certainty that men did not have to die. The whole process was entirely mental. There has never been what the world would call a physical effort in it. I have not strengthened my muscles by exercise; I have not added to my vigor by any form of medication; I have simply reasoned on the great problem of man's existence until I know what he is and how he came to be what he is.

Knowing how he came to be what he is put me in possession of all the knowledge I needed regarding *the law of his growth.*

I never could have acquired this knowledge had I remained in the old race beliefs of physical causation. It was only as I made the transition of thought from the basis of matter to that of mind that the whole thing opened to me, and I knew that *knowing was being*, and that more knowing was greater and more powerful being; and so on until man had climbed up the scale from the negative to the positive pole of life where he saw for himself, with his own intelligence, that he was master of all things including old age and death.

I am not going to write much on this subject. The whole of it is fully given in my other published works. Therefore, I shall again speak of the enterprise that has grown out of our beliefs in the allness of life and the absoluteness of mind.

Before we bought the land of which I have spoken we had to solve the financial question. As we were always talking on the inexhaustible subject of metaphysics, Mr. Post suggested that I write a series of lessons and put them on the market. I did so, and announced the fact through my old paper *The Woman's World*. I charged twenty-five dollars a set for them. They were all in manuscript, and the student was required to copy and return them. The lessons have since then been put into print, and have sold rapidly at a greatly reduced price.

But it seems strange to me, even now, that I should have put them on the market as I did and made such a decided victory of the effort. The first twenty-five dollars that came surprised me, though I was expecting it. Then more orders came, and still more, until I was dazed with success. As a result of this we bought the land and began to improve it. We planted fruit and nut trees; we built a lovely home, and were the happiest people that ever lived I expect. We had money to spend in the effort to assist others. The people about us—though not understanding our ideas in the least—were strongly attracted toward us, and we loved them in return. Always believing in innocent pleasures we gave many entertainments, and enjoyed them ourselves quite as much as our friends did.

But students of metaphysics began to come to us from a distance, and we soon saw that we could not remain in so small a town where the hotels were inadequate to accommodate persons of refinement and culture—such as have always been attracted to the investigation of high thought. It became imperative that we should go somewhere else.

Just six miles from us on the road leading to Atlanta was the celebrated Sweetwater Park with its large and splendid buildings. It was a summer resort, and my classes were held in winter. But the proprietor of the Park consented to open his house to us provided there were enough of us to pay him for the trouble. So we sold our beautiful home and went there with sixty or seventy others, and were there for six months.

But finally we wanted to get away. We had always desired to be close to some large body of water; moreover we had been having many a suppressed longing for Florida. And then, too, a plan for making a sort of nucleus to the great thought we were entertaining had taken root in our minds and was growing rapidly.

Just what we wanted we were not ripe to define; but we had seen that in whatever place we remained long enough to impregnate our surroundings with our views, that everything seemed charged with a strangely magnetic power to draw others to us.

Examining this thing from the standpoint of our foundation statement that *all is mind*, we perceived that it was the actual sprouting of the new and mighty truth relating to man's powers of conquering death, and that all that this truth needed was its establishment in proper soil, and with fostering conditions, in order to take root and grow until it had filled the world with its life-saving influences.

And so presently—without hurry, and also without rest, for we were growing in the strength of the most powerful thought ever conceived by man—we came to Florida.

CHAPTER XXI.

A VISION OF THE DAUNTLESS "I."

I cannot easily forget the night we reached Daytona, Florida. The depot then stood on the bank of the Halifax river; the Palmetto House was some half mile lower down. We took the hack and were driven to it beneath the many palm trees and the wonderful live oaks.

No one has ever been able to describe such a night as that was. The full moon was rising over the trees on the opposite side; the river was a flawless mirror. An unbroken column of light that one might have crossed upon, judging by its appearance, spanned the stream and united the two banks—a bridge of silver. The air was soft, balmy, magnetic. It is no use to talk about the feeling in things being imaginary. I could feel in that atmosphere messages of infinite peace from across the wide ocean that was breaking upon its coast only a mile away. It was an atmosphere purified of personal limitations and personal doubts in its long journey over the beautiful waves;

waves that embossomed the heavens above them no less than the depths below them, and that thus seemed to symbol life in its eternalness.

We spent the entire winter in Daytona, and in the spring returned to Georgia, where, in Atlanta, I started the weekly paper FREEDOM, which was a success from its first issue.

After less than a year in Atlanta, I moved the paper to Boston, and remained there with it for a short time. But the climate of Florida and the clearness and purity of its atmosphere, and the beauty of it, kept drawing me as no other place ever has done. So I came back to find that it was, indeed, the ideal spot I had always been looking for.

Just across the river from Daytona lies a long, narrow stretch of land, washed on its east side by the Atlantic Ocean. A portion of this we purchased and laid off in town lots, and began to improve by grading and shelling the streets and planting palm trees and magnolias and oaks and bays along their borders.

In point of natural advantages the location is simply unsurpassed. The ground is high and dry. Not a drop of stagnant water is to be found upon it. The swamp land, for which Florida is noted, lies farther inland, and no breath from it comes to us by reason of the wind that blows from the ocean. And this wind is not a severe wind as many ocean breezes are. It is just strong enough to temper the heat of summer and keep it deliciously cool. The mercury never rises so high here during the warm weather as it does in any of the northern states; and in the three summers I have spent here, I have not felt the heat as much as I felt it in a few weeks in Boston and Chicago. That the place is lovely in winter is well known; but that there are parts of the state that are even more lovely in summer does not seem to be believed as yet.

The peninsula we are on is one of these rarely favored places. With the Halifax river—which is simply an inlet from the ocean—on one side of us, and the ocean itself on the other side, it is almost as if the breath of eternal purity encompassed us.

And here we are, holding for the manifestation or the outward expression of our highest, our most idealistic hopes. Other persons of similar hopes are joining us here; and the pure natural air is becoming impregnated with a new cast of thought from brains that are no longer steeped in the world's old negative beliefs in the power of disease and death; thought generated from higher reasoning powers than the race has ever used; not higher than it is capable of using, but higher than it is in the habit of using, while under the rule of the deaf, dumb and blind religions of the day. For religions are hitching posts to which the people's brains are tied, and about which they meander round and round in a circle, without advancing a step.

We are the apostles of endless progression through mental unfoldment; we have no creeds; growth is at eternal enemity with creeds, and we are a growing people.

We look abroad and see that life on its present footing is not worth having. The few evanescent and hopelessly ignorant years of adolescence bring us to the point where decay actually begins, even though its manifestations are postponed a few more years. Then comes the breaking up of old age, ending in death.

No wonder that the superficial thinker, deeply discontented with the unsatisfactory brevity of a life that was merely a hint of what might be, should cast about in his brain for another chance of existence under more favorable conditions; and no wonder that, with his ignorance of man's endless power of mental unfoldment, he should hit upon the God-made heaven of the future. It is sufficiently apparent why he did it. In his conception we perceive the dawn; the great truth in its earliest effort to come forth through a mentality not yet grown big enough to give birth to it in its fullness.

"Where there's a will there's a way." To put the broadest construction upon this old adage, knocks down all the bars in existence, and liberates man to the freedom of the universe. We have the will. The will is prophecy of the way. The will could not exist if the way did not. The two are co-relative; they are the Siamese twins of advancement.

To describe briefly our present effort in this place will close the volume.

We are here to learn, and we are here to teach. We have made some marked improvements in the place already, and more are contemplated. It is our intention to build a school that will take pupils of all ages from the baby of the Kindergarten up to the gray-headed student of life's forces and prospects; for the gray head is as much of a baby in his capacity of farther unfoldment on the present side of life as the baby is. Age is no abridgement to any person's chances, if he will only begin to do his own thinking. The awakening of the reasoning powers, and the direction of them toward the investigation of man, is the beginning of the wisdom that saves from death. Mental Science is the study of man. A knowledge of man is a knowledge of the universe; and this knowledge, concentrated in the individual, is power; power over all things.

In the school we mean to establish here, we will employ the best lecturers and teachers on a wide range of subjects; teachers of Oriental History; teachers of Natural History; teachers who are conversant with the rise and decay of the various systems of religious thought; teachers of Evolution; teachers of Mental Philosophy as given forth in the writings of the great metaphysicians of the past; teachers who will sift these various ideas and submit them to the test of the world's latest and best idea, that represented by modern Mental Science. We will establish a Conservatory of Music when we get around to it, and of Art also. Indeed, nothing that will aid in the higher unfoldment will be left out.

Our design, with regard to this place, is to make it an opening from the physical plane of activity—in which all force is limited by what we call the laws of causation—into the limitless realm of mental activity where knowing is being. In other words, we are making a doorway from mortality to immortality through which all may pass—if they choose to learn how to do so—into higher conditions of existence than they now deem possible. It is a doorway from the entire realm of the world's past dim, uncertain, but always belittling, beliefs of itself, into a realm of unbroken personal consciousness of such potency as to destroy utterly all cognition of those shadows upon human intelligence called disease, old age and death.

People cannot make this change without knowing how to do it; and the establishment of this school is to teach them how. It will be a school for the higher education of the race. Teachers will be educated here who will go out in the world to establish branch schools like the parent institution.

When one looks abroad over the entire social organization of the race, he cannot fail to see how the old and effete beliefs of ages of past ignorance are bolstered up.

This system of bolstering up is a perfect thing in its way, and it would be difficult to improve on it. Look at the schools and colleges all over the land for the sole use of perpetuating the old, dead ideas; look at the thousands of churches with their ministers and their wealth, that meet Sunday after Sunday for the exclusive purpose of preventing the birth of free and original thought.

It is true that the persons who contribute to this system, by which the old beliefs are kept operative long after they are dead, are mainly actuated by honest intentions. They are not willfully trying to keep back race intelligence. It is their ignorance of the fact that eternal progress alone is eternal life that makes them so afraid that the people will learn something not endorsed by their forefathers. But it is of small consequence to the sufferers by mistaken methods whether blunders are perpetuated honestly or dishonestly. The thing has got to stop sometime, and consideration for the motive and character of the persons behind the error is not to be weighed in the balance.

Let us imagine that there were schools all over the land for the purpose of teaching people to think, instead of, as now, closing the avenues of original thought within them by cramming them with the thoughts of others; thoughts that failed to save the originators themselves, and that stand comdemned from this very fact. Let us imagine that every church on earth was converted into a scientific lecture hall where the efforts of the best brains would be to bring forth the most comprehensive truths on all the problems of *this* life, and especially the truths bearing upon that problem of all problems—*man*.

How long would it be before the whole world would blossom upward toward the sun of all intelligence in a way to produce the fruit of perfect righteousness (rightness) throughout every department of life, if the vast machinery of the present system of organized effort for the perpetuation of useless creeds were devoted to the attempt to bring forth the undeveloped capacity of the race?

This mighty capacity is the unknown quantity waiting solution in order to bring all the broken cords of life into harmony and establish heaven here on earth.

Who cares for a heaven of the future? Who does not know that so far as practical happiness is concerned that there is no future? We only have what each moment yields. We may look forward toward the future, but the thoughts thus projected out of ourselves weaken us in the present, and bring the future no nearer. To live each moment as it passes is the only way to live; all else is life deferred, ending in death.

But this sketch of my "Search for Freedom" is nearing its close. Have I found what I have been searching for?

Yes I have. I am emancipated from every belief

that stands in the way of my farther development.
The bars to my future progress are down, and this is
freedom in quite a wide sense. If it is not freedom
from all ignorance, it is, at least, freedom to become
free in time.

I have achieved freedom from many things. Whereas my work once enslaved me, the work I now do
makes my happiness. And again in the matter of
burden bearing for others; by the light of Mental
Science I have discoverd that it is no relief to others
to bear their burdens for them, and, therefore, I am
relieved of this form of slavery. There is no crushing
sense of duty on me from any source whatever. I
have learned—this too from Mental Science—that
obedience to the law of attraction supercedes the
slavishness of duty, so that what I do is done in joy
and gladness.

I have learned that happiness is the true watchword of progress, and that as I pursue happiness I
find all desirable things flock to meet me. In this
element of happiness love is generated, and love is the
fruitful mother of every good.

So potent is the effect of this fact that the success
of our undertaking appears to rest upon it. We did
not know when we came here that all the people were

seeking happiness. At least, we did not know that they were seeking it right here and now; but they are. We thought they were denying themselves present happiness for the sake of laying up treasures in heaven; but we were mistaken. It is becoming natural for them to draw away from promises for the future in order to get more out of the present than they have ever yet had; and so the charm of a place that acknowledges the pursuit of happiness as its highest claim is making itself felt far and near; and all the people who come here speak of the health-giving element they find in the atmosphere, and tell how every moment seems fraught with power and blessing.

At present our town is called Sea Breeze; but after a while we shall give it another name. As citizens of the only spot on earth devoted to a search for happiness right here in this world and right now, it surely deserves a better name, and when the improvements we are making shall have ripened into beauty commensurate with the natural beauty of the place, we will accept the name that even now by a sort of general consent is being bestowed upon it—that of "The City Beautiful." The two words "happiness" and "beauty" are our beacon lights. Every effort we are making points straight in their direction. These efforts point over and beyond the clamor that, even as I write, is swelling up from the inharmonious condition of those who are denying this life in order to make preparation for a supposititious better one when this is ended. They are pointing over and beyond the cries of poverty and hard times now ascending day and night in one unbroken wail. They are pointing over and beyond the distress and pain of a thousand deeply grounded beliefs in the God-ordained omnipotence of disease and death; pointing over and beyond all so-called deplorable conditions to the great peace and joy that comes from knowing that all is good; that vital force—life—is self-existent, omnipotent, omniscient, omnipresent, and that it flows into man's statement of being, whether he makes that statement under the delusion of the world's present beliefs in disease, old age and death, or in the knowledge of his power to overcome all his supposed limitations and stand in the freedom of self-creativeness—a veritable god.

This place is not a colony as many persons believe. It is simply an assemblage of individuals who are seeking to individualize themselves more powerfully still through a search for higher truths. We have no business interests which unite us, any more than the citizens of any other village have. Some of us only live here part of the year, having business elsewhere. Freedom has been the object of our search, and freedom is only found in lines of thought and action that are themselves free. Some correspondents would put me under bond to remain here forever, but I will not submit to a bond. I am under the law of attraction; and while I am now so strongly attracted to this place as to feel that I shall never permanently leave it, yet I shall not pledge myself to remain in case the attraction ceased.

And again; the school spoken of is only in embryo as yet. It is an ideal to be built in the future. Let who will come and help externalize this ideal. It is their business as much as mine. I am doing what I can in holding Mental Science classes here every winter; and though this is a good thing to do, yet it is not so good as it would be if others who are competent would take hold and add the other departments of study that would develop the undertaking into a great national institution for an absolutely untrammelled education.

For my part I feel that I can wait. I know that this thing is a growth, and not a building, and that growth is slow. I feel as if the years are all mine, and I need not hurry. Indeed, I know that I am simply in the beginning of the new time, which is carrying the race from under the rule of brute force into that of pure attraction; and I am patient as eternal hope can make me, and happy beyond the power of words to tell.

OUR PUBLICATIONS.

A Blossom of the Century. By Helen Wilmans. Cloth bound, $1.

Oh World, Such as I Have Give I Unto Thee. By Helen Wilmans and Ada Wilmans Powers. Paper, 2 vols., 50 cents each.

The Beginning of Day—A Dream of Paradise. By Helen Wilmans. Paper, 25 cents.

The Home Course in Mental Science. Twenty Lessons. By Helen Wilmans. $5 for the set.

Poverty and Its Cure. By Helen Wilmans. 25 cents.

Metaphysical Essays. By C. C. Post. Paper, 30 cents; cloth, 50 cents.

Our Places in the Universal Zodiac. By W. J. Colville. Paper, 50 cents; cloth, $1.

A History of Theosophy. By W. J. Colville. Paper, 50 cents; cloth, $1.

Freedom. A sixteen-page weekly paper, devoted to the exposition of Mental Science ideas. Price $1 per year.

For any of the above works send to our Publishing House. Address

C. C. POST,
Sea Breeze, Florida.

www.ingramcontent.com/pod-product-compliance
Lightning Source LLC
Chambersburg PA
CBHW020313240426
43673CB00039B/793